Auschwitz & the Holocaust

Eyewitness Accounts from Prisoners & Survivors

Fourth Edition

Disclaimer Notice:

Please note the information contained within this document is for educational purposes only.

Every attempt has been made to provide accurate, up to date and reliable complete information no warranties of any kind are expressed or implied. Readers acknowledge that the author is not engaging in rendering legal, financial or professional advice.

By reading any document, the reader agrees that under no circumstances are we responsible for any losses, direct or indirect, which are incurred as a result of use of the information contained within this document, including – but not limited to errors, omissions, or inaccuracies.

TABLE OF CONTENTS

Introduction

Thank you for purchasing this book, "Auschwitz & the Holocaust: Eyewitness Accounts from Prisoners & Survivors."

World War II was one of the biggest blot marks on the history of the world. Not only did it result in the death of an estimated 55 million to 90 million people, it also led to great losses to the infrastructure of major cities in Europe & East Asia, resulting in an almost stagnation of the economy of several nations.

Some of the reasons why the World War II had almost triple the casualty count of World War I (or The Great War as it is often referred to) were:

(i) Decisive bombing of key cities and major industrial areas that led to heavy casualties.

(ii) The use of nuclear warfare that opened a whole new can of worms.

(iii) The Holocaust, a genocide that was aimed at wiping out the Jew population in the European nations.

These were some of the reasons why the Second World War is said to be the deadliest conflict in the history of mankind.

In this eBook we will concentrate on the Holocaust and the atrocities carried out against the Jews (and some non-Jews).

The "Holocaust" is a term commonly used to describe the extensive and unjust persecution and murder of almost six million Jews by the Nazi regime in Germany, under the leadership of Adolf Hitler. And it was just not the Jews that were persecuted; along with them were persecuted homosexuals, gypsies, Communists, Jehovah's witnesses, and the disabled.

Before being murdered, these people were forced to hide, and if caught, were made to live in terrible conditions in the concentration camps and were often made to do difficult, dangerous and deadly jobs. Many of these unlucky souls were experimented upon. There were chemicals injected into their bodies and they were left to the elements of nature to see how their bodies responded to the extreme circumstances.

Auschwitz was the organizational center of a number of the concentration camps built and controlled by the Third Reich. The concentration camps were situated in the Polish areas that had been annexed by Germany. Historians estimate the number of victims of the death camp at Auschwitz at over one million people, most but not all of them were Jews of Europe. The estimate of people killed by the Nazis in the Holocaust nears 11 million known people, and many are unaccounted for. These deaths occurred all over Europe and the western Soviet Union. There were five other well-known death camps (Belzec, Chelmno, Majdanek, Sobibor, and Treblinka), and the units of the Einsatzgruppen (mobile death squads) and other Nazi units claimed more lives than did the killing center of Auschwitz, yet it is the death factory located just outside of the Polish town of Oswiecim that still casts a shadow of dark fascination seven decades after the end of World War II.

The purpose of this e-book is to provide a brief introduction to the history of Auschwitz. We hope that you will find the information we cover here of interest, and that it will spur you to further study about this horrifying, but important phase of human history that will never fade into the darkness.

Please feel free to share this book with your friends and family. Please also take the time to write a short review on Amazon to share your thoughts. These reviews help others to begin their journey in learning about one of the most important events in world history, and brings awareness to the suffering that happened so many years ago.

Chapter 1: What Was The Holocaust?

Definition of the Holocaust

The Holocaust is a term that is most widely used to describe the mass murder and persecution of the Jews in Germany by Hitler and his Nazi army. This persecution did not just extend to Germany, it also spread through parts of Europe and other countries that were occupied by Hitler at the time.

Many people do not realize that it was not just the Jewish population that was persecuted under the reign of Hitler. Nazis did not limit their persecution to small groups of people, they tortured people for religious, racial and biological reasons. It just so happens that the Jews were the first on the list of targets the Nazis had. Nazis truly believed in their ideology and they believed that certain races, religions and social groups were a threat to the German way of life. They felt that these specific groups were attempting to break down the core of the National Socialist movement.

The Nazi moment was under the impression that the Jewish religion was the enemy and that they must completely irradiate this enemy because they would ultimately be the downfall of the German people. Somehow, they got the idea into their head that the Jewish religion was aiming to drag Christianity down and had the goal of achieving total world domination.

The Nazis had developed a fanatic idea of who the Jews really were. They believed that they were rich, powerful, and in complete control of politics in multiple countries.

The Nazis believed that if they could irradiate the Jews, they would destroy the hold they had on the world. As far as they were concerned, it was war. Jews were a direct enemy of the German people and the aggression from the Second World War, was an effort to combat the Jews, not to eradicate the people of other countries.

Nazi Ideology

What is Nazi ideology and where does it come from? Who comes up with the ideas? Most of these come from mutual hatred, animosity and conflict caused over a thousand years between Christians and Jews. When Judaism first began the Christian Church was hostile towards them. The Jews were persecuted after Christianity became the main religion of states. Jews were not treated equally as a citizen of their country until the modern era when they were no longer persecuted. Christianity had already told and instilled stories that the Jews had killed the Messiah. Stories had been told that Jews were obsessed with gold and would do anything for it. They said that Jesus was betrayed for money by the Jews. These stories were told so much that they became fact to the European culture. In the eighteenth and nineteenth centuries, Jewish persecution ended but the beliefs carried on because the stories had been told for over 100 years.

These stories allowed for the Nazis to extend on them. Also in the nineteenth century there were scientists and anthropologists who came up with the idea of race and developed on it. They came up with the idea that humans were divided into groups called races. These races showed characteristics that were different from each other. They came up with the idea that certain races were more superior than others. Scientists thought that the European race was among the superior race. These people that theorized about race believed there was a race that was the most superior. These supposed Superior German people were called the Aryan volk.

The Rise of the Nazi Party

The German Nationalists took up areas of biology, anthropology, and linguistics that have existed for many years. Unfortunately, when they took these topics, they twisted them to their own interpretation. They believed that Germans were superior and that other people and groups of people were inferior to them. Essentially, they believed they were the chosen race.

They also believed that the people of Jewish faith were their ultimate enemy and that they must be irradiated. Because of this, they aimed to weaken the number of Jewish peoples and basically destroy them through whatever means necessary. They felt they had to get rid of the entire religion before they attempted to take over Germany.

This plan was put into place several decades before WWI.

The Rise of the Nazi Party

During World War 1 there were events that helped the German society. Germany experienced a traumatic loss during World War 1. The Germans were terrified after their loss and were scared that their property, launch class war and nationalist industry would be taken by the Bolsheviks.

After their defeat in World War 1, Germany had a hard time retrieving an audience to share their stories of how the Jews were at fault for their loss. The German people also blamed Jews for Russia having a revolution. During this time Jews were recognized as the enemy. In order to save Germany the people would need to gain power in Germany and expel them. They would also need to reduce any power that they had even destroy them if needed.

The nationalists, who had control of the country at the time, felt that it was increasingly important to save Germany from the power they "felt" the Jewish had. They felt that the Jewish had the power to completely destroy the German government, and that they had the support from many different nations. Of course, this was not the case.

Adolf Hitler had finally found a permanent place for himself. He was extremely intelligent, but also very manipulative. He was mostly self-taught and spent most of his time reading. His passions included reading, debating and arguing. He used what he learned from arguing to fuel his intellectual power. Hitler never did go to college, and his education was not complete, but he made a great debate partner. In fact, Hitler used the ability to debate and argue as a way of expanding his knowledge.

During the WWI, Hitler worked as a spy for Germany. His job was to check for radical groups, infiltrate them, become a member and gain enough status that he was able to give speeches. This allowed him to attract audiences of specific types that the government was looking for. The problem was, he loved the attention entirely too much. He loved being listened to, by anyone, about anything.

When he left the military and gave up being a spy, he joined the radical right-wing movement. Over time, he became the leader of one of the major radical right-wing movements. This party became known over time as the National Socialist German Worker's Party, also known as the Nazi Party.

For years, Hitler and his right-wing party were just a fringe association that never caught anyone's eye. Occasionally, Hitler's party made an appearance when there was some form of economic crisis or strange instability in Germany. They were able to come up with simple solutions that most people overlooked. Eventually, the problems became so large that the country had to blame someone. Thanks to Hitler, the Jews took the hit.

Between 1924 and 1929, Germany was prosperous but verging a Great Depression. Germany was starting to develop the plague of mass unemployment and the people began to rave at the government. While many parties tried to support the people and bring in new jobs, many Germans turned their attention to the Nationalist right-wing parties.

In an electoral contest in 1930, the Nazi party managed to win more seats than was initially thought possible. IN January 1933, Hitler was invited to form a government and take the role of Chancellor of Germany. Bear in mind, this is not the same as the Prime Minister of England. The job of the Chancellor was to maintain rule and order over the Nazi group and its members. He was to control how conservative they were, how radical they become and how far right-winged they went.

Hitler was very smart and in a short period of time, he was able to completely out-maneuver the traditional right-wing nationalists, the conservatives and those who were under the misconception that they could exploit Hitler into doing exactly what they asked of him.

What made it easy for Hitler to out maneuver so many government members was that he had memorized their every move. Shortly after Hitler was placed in office, an arsonist took notice of the German Parliament. It was claimed by the Nazis that the Communists were setting up a coup d'etat.

An act was passed that caused Germany to become a one-party state. This gave all of the power to one dictator. Unfortunately, this dictator was Hitler.

Hitler used his powers as a dictator powers to take down his political enemies. His political enemies were the:

- Communists
- Trade Unions
- Socialists
- Liberals
- and the Jews

Surprisingly, these groups were not at the top of his list of enemies when he became dictator.

During his first year in Nazi power, Hitler began to pull the remaining power from the government and consolidate it into his dictatorship. During this time, disturbances went unnoticed, attacks on Jews went unnoticed, burnings of Synagogues, destruction of Jewish property carried on and Germany became a mess.

The attacks that were carried out during this time were mainly from the "Brown-Shirts, a militia party. While it was unknown to the citizens at the time, this militia stood as the back-bone of the Nazi movement, and it had since the 1920s.

This mass movement consisted of millions of Germans and it was considered by Hitler as the e "street-fighting arm of the Nazi Party." The main job of this militia was to intimidate and rob people to help the Nazi party financially rise to power. During the election of the 1930s, this militia was extremely active.

When Hitler rose to power, this militia assumed that it would have their day in the government, or even in the military. However, they never got this power. They did get influence though.

Hitler allowed them to organize one of the largest boycotts in history, the boycott of the businesses that were owned by Jews in Germany. While the boycott wasn't completely successful, it did cause the businesses significant loss of revenue. It was eventually called off by Hitler and was labeled as stage one of the planed series of acts of intimation. Next came legislation that was directed specifically at the Jewish population. Rather than make them feel unwelcome in Germany, they were made to feel as though they were foreigners in their own land.

In 1930, there were over 1/2 million German-Jewish residents. Most of them had lived in Germany their entire lives, just as their parents before them. They had completely assimilated and become part of the German culture. Other than the way they dressed, you could not tell the religious difference between a Jewish German's attire and another German citizen.

Thousands of these Jews had risked their lives during WWI alongside the German army. Thousands of Jewish people paid the ultimate sacrifice, their lives. Others lost limbs, their mental stability, and their families fighting for Germany. They could not believe that after everything they had sacrificed, Germany would turn their back on them and treat them so terribly.

The Beginning of the Holocaust

At the beginning of Hitler's regime, there was a serious turn for the worse. He was determined to start a war and take over Europe. He removed everyone from power who even resembled a conservative, even if they had been helpful for years on end.

Hitler ensured that his entire regime was determined to impress him. The most ideal solution to introduce his group of military and government personnel was to bash Jews and by helping him pass laws and regulations that were anti-Jew. His overall goal was to make life for the Jewish people in Germany completely unbearable.

Shortly after his regime was started, the military and citizens were permitted to break the windows of Jewish citizens and ransack their homes. By the time morning came, Germany had streets full of broken glass, busted shop windows, and personal items that belonged to people of the Jewish population. Even worse, synagogues were wrecked, burned and left in rubble.

Shortly after, the Nazi army took a large number of Jewish men into custody for no reason. They were sent directly to be inhumanely imprisoned in concentration camps. The main reason was to reduce the male population, which limited the amount of resistance the religion could produce.

While they expected some resistance, the leadership of the Nazis were not content with the way the world responded to the "Night of Broken Glass." There were obvious protests the world over, which seriously upset the German military and government.

Since some German leaders were not consulted about the plans, they felt extremely upset. They knew it would have a serious impact on Germany's economy since there were so many Jewish businesses that contributed to the tax revenue.

However, they felt that they could make a profit off of all of the seized assets, businesses, properties and personal items that were left behind when the Jews were taken to concentration camps or fled.

Soon after, freed Jews controlled the SS, one of the most powerful military installments in the area. Since the SS took charge of immigration, they were pretty much free to go anywhere they pleased; at least until the power they had was taken away from them by the German government. Since the government was under the assumption that the largest enemy they had were Jews, and believed that they were involved in conspiracy world-over, the government believed they must be destroyed.

Judaism became known as a virus, so people were no longer accepted into the typical "Aryan life." They had become a humanitarian threat and it was time that they were destroyed.

Between the concentration camps, the gas-chambers, and the brutal torture that the Jews were suffering, World War II began to develop. The world demanded that the war against the Jews be stopped and stood together in removing Hitler from his "throne."

World War II

The Jews had unfortunately been taken over by one of the most brutal and vicious regimes in the world, the Nazis. In September of 1939, Nazis began to take over Europe. They began with Germany and made their way to Poland. This was the trigger of World War II.

Once Germany had taken over Western Poland, they begin setting up trains with an anti-Semitic mission. Their main focus was the Jewish population. Their first target was cities that contained the largest number of Jews. They began moving the Jewish people to ghettos. They were stripped of rights, money and any assets that they did own.

Because of the attention they drew, they began losing their jobs, triggering an abundance of unemployment and extreme poverty. All of this lead to a sequence of death and disease spreading throughout the ghettos that the Jews were assigned to live in.

As famine and sickness took over the population, the Jewish that were not imprisoned began to leave for Austria and the Czech lands. However, even if you do not count the Jews that were locked up in concentration camps, or the ones who had been killed in the gas chambers, there were still over 500 thousand Jews trapped in Poland alone.

The Jews that were left behind in Poland were despised greatly, compared to those that were trapped in Germany, especially if they were extremely religious.

Because of the dress code that was given by their religion, they stood out more than any other religions. This became even more of a reality when their everyday clothing was taken away and they were given threadbare rags to wear.

The polish population was told that everything about Judaism was terrible and horrible. This is when the street violence really began.

There was a huge number of Jewish people killed on the street and these murders were taking place on an unbelievably large scale. Even though the killings were being carried out by the military and by civilians, they were not systematic. At this point, everyone in Poland understood that Jewish people were fair game and that they would not be prosecuted for killing them. They just knew that the Jewish population was making life more difficult for everyone involved.

According to Hitler's Army, you can execute a Jew or take their property and nobody's going to care. In their eyes, you are working towards the Fuhrer and doing exactly what Adolf Hitler needs by oppressing Jews, making their lives hopeless, and taking their homes and riches.

Take It All Over

In early 1940. the German's managed to fulfill their goal of taking over Western Europe in a victory that gave them power over an even larger Jewish population.

Unfortunately, since:

- Over 300,000 Jews escaped to France
- Over 140,000 Jews escaped to the Netherlands
- Over 140,000 Jews escaped to Belgium
- Over 60,000 Jews escaped to other areas

They were no longer safe. This means that Nazis regained control of more than 640,000.

After a short period of time, the Jews who were once save were forced to live by the same legislation that Germany handed down.

To make matters worse, a huge anti-Jewish revolution was flying through the population in many countries. They were stereotyped and treated worse than you would ever treat a stray dog.

Friction Worsens

In the country of Poland, there had always been a tenseness between the Jewish population and the non-Jewish population.

While no one really sought out Jews for persecution, they really did not blend with the other Polish population. There were a lot of differences in the population divide and the situation brought on by the Jewish persecution just made matters worse. In the best of situations, the Polish were indifferent to the Jews, meaning that as long as they stayed to themselves, there was not a problem.

The attack of Russia in 1941 changed all of this. German policy began to encourage the Polish to expel the Jews from their country and those who would not leave, permission was given to make their lives difficult.

Basically, it was made impossible for Jews to thrive, or even to live in the conditions they were provided. Unfortunately, there were very few countries who would accept Jews and those who would were cooperating with the Nazi army.

Before the beginning of World War II, many countries tightened their immigration restrictions to avoid being bombarded by refugees. After the war began, many boarders were completely closed. At this point, Jews were stuck in Germany, the one place they didn't want to be. Their only other option was to flee to South America, but getting a visa was almost impossible.

An Ultimate Solution

1941's summer months brought about change in the Nazi's hierarchy. Even historians do not know exactly when it began and it is extremely difficult to find a document that marks the change or how the change began.

However, at this time, the Nazi moment changed its policy from removing Jews from their homes in the areas that they controlled. The change that took place was that they were no longer putting Jews in concentration camps and working them to death, they actually began murdering them in mass numbers. They were attempting to annihilate them completely. Their goal, to kill off all existing Jews.

The invasion looks to have began with Russia and Germany's army was followed behind by a group of 4 specialized mobile task groups.

Each group had its own jobs, including compiling intelligence, preventing resistance, capturing communists, and anyone working with Soviet states. Others were tasked with killing Jews. Together, these groups were called the Einsatzgroupen.

The first set of large scale shootings began in 1941, during the summer. The began sometime between the invasion on June 22, 1941 and August's end that same year.

While the Einsatzgroupen originally began killing men, they eventually began killing women and children as well, turning the entire situation into pure annihilation.

This decimation started with shooting en masse in countries like Russia and eventually made its way back to Poland. Over time, it made its way to Western Europe.

Jews were eventually restricted to public squalor over a year and a half. Over this time, there was mass suffering, starvation, and unemployment.

However, over time, the Jews began turning the ghettos into productive centers where they could produce many of the things needed by the German army.

Hitler and the people around him started seeing these Jewish ghettos in a different way. They began using them to discard the unwanted German people into, along with the existing residents.

The mixed population was forced compensate for this overflow. The local people who were considered weak, or unable to work were systematically and brutally slaughtered. At this time, it was not just the Nazis who were killing off the weak Jews who were unable to contribute, but local inhabitants began killing them off as well to reserve resources.

The noted killings were done by using poisonous gas, shooting, strangling and deadly beatings. The poisonous gas was pushed into apartments through hoses that were attached to box trucks containing gas canisters.

This technology was invented as a way to mass execute the Germans. The number of people that were killed injured the German army by this second war of the world. This is because the start of the second world war began in 1939 and many of the men that they were depending on were either dead, mentally disabled, or physically disabled.

Many of the men, women and children who survived were stuck in sanatoriums or asylums because of the effects of the gas. These people were considered unworthy of eating, and many were left to die. By allowing these people to die, they were able to empty space and create room in hospital for wounded German army soldiers.

During this time, over 70,000 were horribly murdered in gas chambers, with the use of gas vans and through shooting and beating them to death, regardless of age or sex. All of this happened during the years of 1939 and 1940.

At the end of 1941 and the beginning of 1942, history becomes a little scattered about what actually happened. The Nazis attempted to destroy the Soviet Jewish population and aimed to get rid of as much of them as humanly possible. Their means of wiping them out, mass murder. Soon after they wiped out the Jewish population in the Soviet Union, their goal was to wipe the Jewish population out of Poland, and eventually, Europe itself.

To make it possible, massive death camps were built.

Extermination Camps:

To achieve this massive extermination, death camps were built. These locations were meant for absolutely nothing but wiping out populations of people that the Nazis did not want to deal with or felt were a threat.

These places were located at Belzec, Sobibor and Treblinka. These are the three camps that destroyed the majority of the European Jewish population.

Another camp, located at Majdanek is the most famous. It is known as Auschwitz-Birkenau. While it was not originally built as a death camp, it eventually became one. The original purpose of this camp was a concentration camp, where people were forced to do manual labor, sometimes until they were worked to death.

Between 1930 and 1941, Germans systematically tortured tens of thousands of Polish citizens and Jews. In 1941, the camp was expanded and a second camp was built. A gas-chamber was built, which used a cyanide gas Zyklon-B. mixture. With the addition of the gas-chamber, the targeted people were transported to the camp with the sole purpose of being killed.

Only a small fraction of each trainload of people were chosen for manual labor. Even though manual labor may sound better than the gas-chamber, it was really just a slower, more painful form of death.

Prisoners were not provided enough food and were treated in the most brutal fashion you could ever imagine. Between the start of summer 1942 and the end of 1943 over 3,000,000 Jews were brutally murdered for no reason other than their religion.

Between the winter of 1942 and the winter of 1943, the Germans were finding it harder to find Jewish people to feed their concentration camps. This was due to several reasons.

- Many of the Jewish Allies began to get nervous about the war the Germans were trying to start.
- The Jews had become wiser and became better at hiding, fleeing, and fighting back.

In 1943 there was an uprising of the Jews that sparked a massive resistance all over Europe. Men in the Jewish ghettos began to fight back against Germans who came to deport them to Poland. Massive numbers of Jewish people fled to hiding places in Russia and formed their own underground army.

In France, members of the Jewish underground army began uprising against German soldiers in small numbers. Because of these uprisings, the deportation train stopped completely. Belgium freed several hundred Jews that were initially meant to be deported to Nazi death camps.

Beginning in 1943, countries began to gain more support for the Jewish community and the areas where they lived. These countries started speaking out in anger against Germans because of the treatment of the Jews and many countries that supported the Germans began backing out, and it appeared that the Germans would lose the war.

While the victory was late and entirely too many people died before a solution was found, the Jewish people pulled off a win.

Chapter 2: Auschwitz

Auschwitz, now known as a major a physical reminder of the holocaust, is located in Oswiecium, which is outside of Cracow, Poland. The original reason that Hitler chose this location is because it is a centralized location where it could be reached through any mode of transportation, except walking. Because of this, the area they controlled. It could be reached through any system of roads and railways in the areas that were patrolled regularly.

Prior to WWII, this area was occupied by people of the Jewish religion. These people were typically artisan and merchants who were just trying to make a living. The Jews who made a living here made up over half of the town's working class population. After the Holocaust was over, many people felt that the town of Oswiecim would avoided by tourists, especially those of persecuted faiths. The presence of Auschwitz-Birkenstock, since it was the largest concentration camps controlled by the Nazis, and was also the main camp used as an extermination center.

The geographical size of Auschwitz was not the only problem faced by the area. The main problem that was faced is due to the fact that Jews were transported from every portion of Europe that Hitler had control over. The selection process was not rigorous, you simply had to be Jewish, Polish, or have a physical appearance that did not match what Hitler felt was ideal. Depending on the results from the selection processing, many of them were many were completely overlooked for manual labor, and were sent directly to the gas chamber. Soon after they were horribly gassed to death, they were cremated.

In this book, you will read many testimonies that are graphic, disturbing, but necessary. These are the testimonials of survivors who miraculously made it out of the camp alive. When we use the name "Auschwitz" we are directly referring to a camp that can be described as nothing more than a center of torture, a center of horror that could never really be imagined, unless you lived through it. Even today, there is an aura of horror and evil that emanates from the walls of this horrible place.

While it may be easy to act as though Auschwitz is a different planet, it is not. It was made here, on earth. It is a massive complex of buildings that were created by humans in an effort to execute other people for no justified reason, and in the cruelest, most industrialized manner possible.

How They Kept Prisoners In

Auschwitz was outlined by high barbed-wire fences that were connected to an electric current. These fences were heavily guarded by soldiers that were armed with high powered rifles and machine guns.

Many people who made it out of this camp recount the sound of the razor-wire fences howling with electricity, but they also felt that the ground itself moaned from the reminiscence of the fallen victims.

By March of 1942, heavyhearted trains that were carrying Jews started arriving at Auschwitz daily, and sometimes several times per day. Every train that came in carried thousands of human beings who originated in the lower income areas of Eastern Europe.

Auschwitz - What Really Happened

Not only did the trains entering Auschwitz bring in Jews the lower income areas of Eastern Europe., they also brought them in from other European countries as well.

More than 1 1/2 million people were brutally murdered n the horrible, inescapable gas chambers in Auschwitz and at least 90% of them were Jewish. The remaining 10% can be broken down into Polish, Soviet POWs, other religious sects, homosexuals and random members of the population.

The majority of Nazi victims originated in from all over Europe and nearby countries. These people were completely unaware of where they were going, or what fate they would suffer once they got there. They were treated worse than animals and they arrived at the camp completely exhausted. The majority of these poor souls never had the opportunity to enter the camp, they simply passed it on their march to the gas chamber, where they met their untimely end.

These lucky few that became prisoners, had their heads shaved, lived in stripped uniforms and had their heads shaved. They were used for tortured laborers and anything that differentiated their gender was removed. Their name was taken away from them, and they were known only by the numbers that were tattooed on their arms.

Even though the Nazi guards took time out to terrorize and dehumanize prisoners, many Jews retained they were stripped of any human dignity and what little humanity they had left. They suffered through lack of clothing, lack of shoes, lack of medical care, and even through unbearable conditions. To survive, they maintained support systems, friendships, and groups to help one another survive the horrible conditions they were being forced to live in.

Auschwitz: Slave Labor and Extermination

After the camp was created, the city of Oswiecim underwent a complete name change. It was now known as Auschwitz by the Germans and those who supported them. Shortly after, the name of the city changed, the camp became known as Auschwitz as well. This "camp" functioned as a forced labor facility, and in a very short time it became the most massive Nazi concentration camp known to man.

When the camp was originally started, it was a relocation facility for the Polish, by German soldiers. The majority of prisoners were considered the elite from Poland and were they were sent there because of their views and their outcries against the changes the Germans were trying to instate. Among these people were groups of resistance members as well as their officers.

Over time, Nazis felt that other groups were becoming a threat. In 1942, people of the Jewish faith and many SS doctors who were capable of manual labor, were shipped to and registered for the camp.

More than 1/2 of all of the prisoners who were registered died from starvation, working harder than the human body was meant to and the brutal torment that echoed through the camp. Other culprits were living conditions that no human could survive, diseases that rampaged through the camp, and inhumane medical treatments and experiments.

Over a number of years, the original torture facility was expanded and ended up consisting of three sections:

Auschwitz I

Auschwitz II - Birkenau

Auschwitz III- Monowitz

... and 40 sub-camps

Most of the people who were sent to Auschwitz met their death shortly after arrival by means of the horrific gas chamber. When the war finally ended, the SS started dismantling the buildings that were known for torturing and killing so many innocent people. They began destroying documents that explained what occurred at the location.

The prisoners who were capable of walking away on their own free will were taken to the depths of the Reich. Those who were forced to stay were then liberated by the Soldiers of the Red Army in January of 1945.

Auschwitz-Birkenau was later turned into a museum by the Polish Parliament. The two portions of Auschwitz I and Auschwitz II, were deemed museums on July 2, 1947.

Concentration Camp Guards

It was not uncommon to see male guards paroling the grounds of the various concentration camps that the Nazis had built. Given that it was the 1930s, males were expected to guard large populations of people who could easily upraise and take over the camp, leaving pretty much every guard and staff member dead, or near dead.

Many people were, and are still under the impression that the only danger that was faced by prisoners in concentration camps were angry men. Unfortunately, there was something even more menacing lurking in the shadows of concentration camps, female guards who had to prove that they were just as tough as the male guards.

As the male officers patrolled the grounds, many of the female guards went completely unnoticed, but they were there in pretty strong numbers.

While it was well known then, now, the sheer population of women who served in the SS Nazi Army was actually pretty high given that it occurred in the 1930's.

At any point, on any given day, there were at least 170 female SS guards on the grounds at Auschwitz. Keep in mind, this is only one of the dozens of concentration camps that the Nazis had built.

You may be wondering why women were allowed to serve as guards for the concentration camps. The truth is that the depth of brainwashing that all Germans went through as children made it perfectly okay for men and women alike to be violent toward, and murder those who did not fit the stereotypical

German lifestyle. Since so many of these guards were killed, died when the camps were overthrown, and others died of old age, there is no way to complete an accurate clinical study on the depth at which these people were brainwashed.

It is noted many times in various history books that unlike the Germans, the rest of the world had a different view of gender roles. Because of this, there were very few women charged with war crimes, and those who were charged, could have easily become the worlds worst nightmares if they had been let go.

Some of the female guards were so terrible to prisoners and the public alike that their names still ring through the history books. Many of them were put to death after being convicted of crimes involving civil war, while others served their entire lives in prison.

Among these female guards, the most noted were:

Irma Grese   (hanged December '45)

Elizabeth Lupka   (hanged January '47)

Johanna (Juana) Bormann   (hanged December '45)

Greta (Mueller) Bosel   (hanged May '47)

Elizabeth Volkenrath   (hanged December '45)

Elisabeth Marschall   (hanged May '47)

Gerda Steinhoff   (hanged July '46)

Maria Mandel   (hanged January '48)

Elisabeth Becker   (hanged July '46)

Therese Brandel   (hanged January '48)

Jenny Wanda Barkmann   (hanged July '46)

Ruth Closius-Neudeck	(hanged July '48)
Wanda Klaff	(hanged July '46)
Emma Zimmer	(hanged September '48)
Dorothea Binz	(hanged May '47)
Ida Schreiter???	(hanged September '48)

Out of all of the female guards that patrolled the grounds, the most remembered female guard was Irma Grese.

When WWII began, the British noticed that nearly 3,600 women were employed in concentration camps and out of these women, 60 women faced War Crimes because of their actions between 1945 and 1949, including the women listed above. The actions of the women listed here were so brutal that their crimes outweighed almost every man who worked in a concentration camp.

At the same time, nearly 500 men stood trial for war crimes and crimes against many of the most powerful countries in the world. Nearly 500 war criminals were immediately sentenced to death and were executed. Since they were convicted of war crimes, many of them were hanged, which was the normal procedure at the time.

Chapter 3: Auschwitz and the Purpose of Each Camp and Sub Camp

Women's Concentration Camps

Not many people are aware of the fact in the first 6 years since the existence of Third Reich, many women were subjected to concentration camp. The women were taken to concentration camps with male representatives of SS (like Nordheim) who used to control and watch over .Thanks to the fact that the terror was in an up-rise since 1939 spring , it was important that a different female cell for prisoners were created. The Ravensbruck was founded by the Nazis, it was called the FKL or Frauen Konzentrationslager and was basically a women's concentration camp in the Northern side of Berlin. Initially, the camp was made to accommodate as many as 10,000 people. In this Northern Berlin Camp, there were special SS female guards who used to oversee the prisoners and ensure that the perform the required labor and also oversee that they adhered to the camp rules and regulations. Most of these SS female guards saw this as a lucrative job with high pay, many saw them as a unique job opportunity to break free from their home also a few saw this post as a job on the newspaper and responded to it. However, getting the job was not simple, they had to undergo an entrance exam and only on clearing they got to sign a contract with SS Post that they had to undergo few months of rigorous training in Ravensbruck. Though these women guards wore SS uniforms and were on their payroll, they did not enjoy the same set of rights as the male members. All outer watch posts of the camp and leadership positions were only reserved for the male members.

About 1,30,000 females were sent to this camp during the years 1939 to 1945, amongst them as many as 90,000 female died due to illness, lack of food and brutal treatment of the female guards. Many of these female guards who were trained in Ravensbruck got employed at other concentration camps like Lublin-Majdanek, Auschwitz, Plaszów and so on.

Right before WWII broke out, Hitler organized a speech directed at his Generals of "Wehrmacht" at Obersalzberg. In his speech, he made it clear that speed and brutality was important, pointing out how Genghis Khan happily ordered millions to death, including children. He felt that the point of war was to annihilate the enemy by whatever means necessary. His goal was to eliminate and depopulate anyone who originated in Poland or spoke the Polish language and to settle Poland with Germans. In his words:

"Only in this way will we gain the territory we need in order to live..."

Poland was invaded by the German army shortly after, on Hitler's orders, as part of one of the massive operational groups. The most noted groups were Service Police and Security. These groups are noted to be involved in crimes such as arresting people in mass quantities, mass executions, and more. The reason these crimes were carried out were due to rules and laws set forth by Hitler, who wanted to eliminate those involved in social activism, Polish intelligentsia, Jews and their clergy. The prisons were taking in too many prisoners, which forced Hitler to come up with a plan to hide away any, and everyone, who stood against his ruling.

At the end of 1939, the Nazi control and Hitler developed a project that ultimately became the concentration camp of Auschwitz. This plan was developed to decrease the amount of time it took to eradicate the Polish. The camp was officially established that following June on the 14th. The location of this camp was at the fork created by two rivers This location was chosen because it was secluded from the rest of the world, and the things that were happening at this camp could easily be hidden from the public eye. It also linked up with the railroad General Government headquarters.

Nazi Concentration Camps

Camp Name	Camp Type
Alderney	Labor camps
Amersfoort	Transit camp and prison
Arbeitsdorf	Labor camp
Auschwitz-Birkenau	Extermination and labor camp
Banjica	Concentration camp
Bardufoss	Concentration camp
Bełżec	Extermination camp
Berga an der Elster (Berga, Thuringia)	Labor camp; Buchenwald sub-camp
Bergen-Belsen	Collection Point
Berlin-Marzahn	"rest place" then labor camp for Roma
Bernburg	Collection point
Bogdanovka	Concentration camp
Bolzano	Transit
Bredtvet	Concentration camp
Breendonk	Prison and labor camp
Breitenau	"Early Wild Camp", then Labor Camp
Buchenwald	Labor Camp
Chełmno (Kulmhof)	Extermination Camp
Crveni krst	Concentration camp
Dachau	Labor camp

Drancy	Internment camp, transit
Falstad	Prison camp
Flößberg (Frohburg)	Labor camp; Buchenwald sub-camp
Flossenbürg	Labor camp
Fort de Romainville	Prison and transit camp
Fort VII (Poznań)	Concentration, detention, transit
Fossoli	Prison and transit camp
Grini	Prison Camp
Gross-Rosen	Labor Camp
Herzogenbusch (Vught)	Prison camp
Hinzert	Labor camp
Jägala	Concentration camp
Janowska (Lwów)	Collection point and sub-camp
Jasenovac concentration camp	Labor camp
Kaiserwald (Mežaparks)	Ghetto; transit, labor & extermination camp
Kaufering/Landsberg	Extermination camp for Jews, Serbs, Croats and Roma
Kauen (Kaunas)	Labor camp
Kemna	Labor camp
Klooga	Ghetto and internment camp
Koldichevo	Early concentration camp
Langenstein-Zwieberge	Labor camp
Le Vernet	Labor camp
Majdanek	Buchenwald sub-camp

(KZ Lublin)	
Malchow	Internment camp
Maly Trostenets	Extermination camp
Mauthausen-Gusen	Labor Camp
Labor and Transit camp	Transit Camp
Mechelen	Labor Camp; sub-camp
Mittelbau-Dora	Labor Camp; Extermination camp
Mittelsteine	Labor Camp
Natzweiler-Struthof (Struthof)	Prison and labor camp
Neuengamme	Concentration Camp
Niederhagen	Labor and concentration camp; Buchenwald sub-camp
Oberer Kuhberg	Early concentration camp
Ohrdruf	Collective point
Oranienburg	Labor Camp
Osthofen	Labor Camp for Women
Płaszów	Police Detainment Camp
Ravensbrück	Labor Camp
Risiera di San Sabba (Trieste)	Extermination Camp
Sachsenhausen	Labor Camp
Sajmište	Transit and labor camp
Salaspils (Kirchholm)	Extermination camp
Skrochowitz (Skrochovice)	Labor; Transit camp
Sobibór	Labor camp
Soldau	Transit camp and Ghetto
Stutthof	Extermination camp

Theresienstadt (Terezín)	Concentration and Transit Camp
Treblinka	Labor and Extermination Camp
Vaivara	Concentration and transit camp
Warsaw	Labor and extermination camp
Westerbork	Transit camp

Nazi Sub-camps

Name Of Subcamp	Number of Prisoners
Harmense (Geflügelfarm)	About 150 prisoners
Budy (Wirtschaftshof)	700-800 prisoners
Babitz (Wirtschaftshof)	About 340 prisoners
Birkenau (Wirtschaftshof)	More than 200 prisoners
Rajsko (Gärtnerei)	About 300 female prisoners
Plawy (Wirtschaftshof)	About 200 prisoners
Golleschau	About 1,000 prisoners
Jawischowitz	More than 2,500 prisoners
Chelmek (Aussenkommando)	About 150 prisoners
Monowitz Buna-Werke	10,223 prisoners in three IG Farben locations as of 17 January 1945.
Eintrachthütte	1,374 prisoners
Neu-Dachs	More than 3,500 prisoners
Fürstengrube	700-1,200 prisoners
Janinagrube (Gute Hoffnung)	877 prisoners
Lagischa	About 1,000 prisoners
Günthergrube	300-600 prisoners
Gleiwitz I	About 1,300 prisoners

Laurahütte	1,000 prisoners
Blechhammer	609 prisoners
BobrekAbout	50-213 prisoners and about
Gleiwitz II	More than 1,000 prisoners
Sosnowitz II	About 900 prisoners
Gleiwitz III	450-600 prisoners
Hindenburg	About 400-500 female prisoners and about 70 prisoners
Trzebinia	600-800 prisoners
Tschechowitz (Bombensucherkommando)	About 100 prisoners
AlthammerAbout	500 prisoners
BismarckhütteAbout	200 prisoners
CharlottengrubeAbout	1,000 prisoners
NeustadtAbout	400 female prisoners
Tschechowitz-VacuumAbout	600 prisoners
Hubertushütte	200 prisoners
FreudenthalAbout	300 female prisoners
LichtewerdenAbout	300 female prisoners
SosnitzAbout	30 prisoners
Porombka (SS-Hütte)	About 50 prisoners and about 10 female prisoners
AltdorfAbout	20 prisoners

RadostowitzAbout	20 prisoners
Kobier (Aussenkommando)	About 150 prisoners
Brünn	250-150 prisoners
Sosnowitz (I)	About 100 prisoners
Gleiwitz IV	About 500
Kattowitz (Sonderkommando)	10 prisoners
Bauzug	About 500

Chapter 4: Origins

The town of Oswiecim, Poland, lies in the south of Poland, thirty miles from the historic city of Krakow, and just north of the Czech and Slovak Republics. The German pronunciation of the town's name is Auschwitz, and it is by that name that the world took note of the town. The name of the town pulls on the heartstrings of people who know what happened there. It brings tears to people's eyes, especially those who suffered through the torture and those who lost loved ones in this horrible camp of torture.

The town of Oswiecim was founded in the eleventh century, and like the nation that it lies within, the town and surrounding area was controlled by many different kingdoms, nobles, and nations throughout its history. Oswiecim was controlled by the Prussians (the large German state that became the core of modern Germany in the 19th century), the Austro-Hungarian Empire, and the Swedes. It sat on the invasion routes of many armies moving north, south, east, and west. The town was destroyed a number of times, first by the Mongols in the 1200s and later, a number of times by fire. It had a rich and varied history of nearly 800 years. Yet, virtually the entire world knows of the town not for those eight centuries, but for a four and a half year period in the middle of the 20th century.

History is filled with irony. In this case, the irony is that Casimir III the Great, King of Poland from 1333-1370, and whose seat of power was Krakow, the largest city near Oswiecim, was one of the most tolerant monarchs of the Middle Ages. In a time when many other Christian kings and nobles were filled with superstitious anti-Semitism, Casimir relaxed previous laws passed against the Jews and promoted Jewish immigration into his kingdom.

Sadly, as the centuries passed, that tolerance in Poland lessened, and by the 1920s, when Poland became an independent nation once again, many Poles were anti-Semitic. Still, this should not be taken to mean that all Poles were. When WWII broke out in 1939, there were an estimated 3 million Jews in Poland, out of a total population of nearly 35 million. Other minorities in Poland were Ukrainians, Russians, Germans, Roma/Sinti (commonly known as gypsies), and a variety of others, which made up another 10 million people altogether.

The history and basis for anti-Semitism is discussed in depth in our other e-book, entitled "The Holocaust – An Introduction," and we encourage you to download the volume for an introduction to Holocaust history as a whole. For our purposes here, we can say that anti-Semitism grew from religious misunderstanding and misinterpretation, the inherent prejudice that seems to follow all minorities or immigrant cultures within a larger society, the fear and misunderstanding of the different and alien, resentment on the basis of belief, which exaggerated the role of the Jews in banking, government and culture, plus later 19th and early 20th century pseudo-scientific ideas about race which proclaimed the white race (particularly those elements of it from northern Europe) superior to all others on Earth.

When Hitler came to power in 1933, the Nazi regime began to incrementally put limitations on the civic and private lives of Jews in Germany. In the years before they came to power, the Nazi paramilitary organization, the SA (for "Sturmabteilung," better known to history as "storm troopers"), would assault and denigrate Jews and those suspected of being Jews in the major cities of Germany where the Nazis had a following.

When they came to power, the Nazis organized a boycott against Jewish businesses and book burnings to protest what they believed to be excessive Jewish influence in German culture, which was over-exaggerated.

In 1934, the SA was purged by an elite smaller unit – a more ruthless, efficient, highly organized unit, the SS (the "Schutzstaffel," or "protection echelon"). The SS was the umbrella organization under which all of the police units in Germany eventually came under, and they gathered information on all the Jews of Germany.

In 1935, the Nuremberg Laws were passed, which were the first in a series of edicts that began to limit German Jews' social, professional, and personal lives. Jews were forbidden to marry Jews, have extramarital sexual relations with them, hire Germans to work for them in most professional areas, practice the law, treat Germans as doctors, etc. Over the next few years, German Jews were completely isolated and removed from German society.

In 1938, a Polish Jew studying in Paris, whose family had been living in Germany since 1911, received a letter from his sister telling him that she and the rest of his family had been forcibly repatriated to Poland, losing everything in the process. Having suffered years of abuse at the hands of the Nazis, Herschel Grynszpan walked into the German Embassy in Paris and shot a German diplomat to death. This was just the excuse the Nazis needed, and on the night of November 9th and 10th, Nazi party members in plainclothes, along with gangs of teenage Hitler Youth members and others, broke the windows of Jewish homes and businesses all over Germany. They also assaulted Jews in the streets, killing nearly 100, and set fire to hundreds of synagogues all over Germany and Austria, which had been annexed to Germany earlier in the year. This night, known by its German name "Kristallnacht," or "Night of Broken Glass," marks the beginning of the Holocaust in the eyes of many historians and those of the Jewish faith as well.

When the war broke out in 1939 there were some within the Nazi Party that believed that the Jews of Europe should be killed. At that point in time, these people were a minority. Most believed the Jews should be deported from Germany or lands under Nazi control, but two factors prevented that from happening. First, with each conquered territory, the Germans absorbed greater numbers of Jews, exactly the opposite of what they wanted. Secondly, with the start of the war, areas of the world that the Germans had wanted to send the Jews, such as Madagascar, were now impossible to access because of boarder restrictions.

With the conquest of western Poland in 1939, and the rest of the country from the Soviet Union in 1941, the Nazis began a process of concentrating the

Jews in specific areas of Polish towns and cities. These were the "ghettos," and each of them, while different in some ways, had many similarities.

These towns and cities were grossly overcrowded. Sanitation facilities were overworked or non-existent. Food, supplied by the Germans, or smuggled in through the fenced, walled, and barbed wire borders of the ghettos, was grossly inadequate, contaminated, and considered scraps and people began to starve to death. The most vulnerable were the children and elderly, who had weakened immune systems and did not have the ability to fight off the germs and bacteria that were in this inadequate food. Drinking water was also in short supply. Medical supplies were virtually impossible to find, and disease and infection were rife. Many who survived the horrendous food that was provided fell ill to the disease and infection that was spreading like wildfire throughout the Jewish community. Many works of literature and history have been written on the ghettos in Poland, and we ask that if you are interested in this facet of Holocaust history, you continue your study by delving into them.

When the Germans attacked eastward into eastern Poland, the Baltic countries, and the Soviet Union on June 22nd, 1941, millions more Jews came under their control. This was in addition to those from the western nations of France, Belgium, Holland, Luxembourg, Denmark, and Norway that they had already conquered. In Western Europe, partially to keep a less anti-Semitic population calm, the Germans did not form ghettos, but they surely enacted anti-Semitic policies throughout their territory. When the Nazis decided on a policy of extermination later in the war, Western European Jews were rounded up quickly, sometimes held in camps or specially designated areas for a short time, and then loaded on trains to the extermination centers that had been built in Poland and other areas of the territory.

It was with the attack eastward that the Nazis, who were already in many ways pushed to the limit of the resources they were willing to allot for the maintenance of the Jewish populations under their control, began a policy of mass killing to reduce the number of Jews they had to care for on a regular basis. The main reasons behind this was to reduce the amount of money they were putting out to feed them. Over time, the reasoning became much more self serving.

At first, this killing took the place of large-scale massacres, done by shooting large groups of Jews and burying them in mass graves. These massacres were sometimes performed with the aid of collaborators and nationalist anti-Semitic paramilitaries, especially in the Baltic states of Latvia and Lithuania, and the Ukraine. In 1941 and 1942, the Nazi "Einsatzgruppen," or "Special Action Squads," slaughtered just over a million men, women, and children, sometimes in the most brutal and public ways.

These massacres, while eliminating the Nazis' need to house the Jews, had a number of unintended effects: they were very public and influenced, to a degree, resistance to Nazi rule. However, it must be said that many in the conquered territories not only aided the Nazis in rounding up Jews to be killed and took part in the killing themselves, but some came out *just to watch*. Some of those watching the slaughter were German soldiers and civilians, some of whom took pictures of what they were seeing and sent them home – something the Nazi Party did not want to have happen as it drew worldwide attention to something they were trying to keep as secret as possible … well, as much as you can keep mass killings a secret.

The mass killing, such as the image shown above, also took a toll on some of the men who were committing the murders. Suicides began to happen, alcoholism skyrocketed, and comments in letters to family back home in Germany increased. Another way needed to be found by the Nazis to "deal" with the Jews under their control.

In the fall of 1941, commanders at German camps in Poland began to experiment with the idea of using gas, rather than bullets, to kill the Jews of the conquered territories. The gas idea originally developed from a program, which was started in Germany in 1939. This was the "T-4" program, which was the killing of what the Nazis called "Life unworthy of life." To the Nazis, this meant the mentally disabled, and those with severe birth defects. At various sanatoriums around the country, tens of thousands of German citizens from children to the elderly were put to death by lethal injection or by gas. One of the SS engineers that worked on creating gas chambers at the T-4 facilities, Lorenz Hackenholt, later designed and used the gassing facilities at Belzec, and later the Sobibor and Treblinka death camps. Other SS personnel, including guards, doctors, and officers, later manned the death camps and supervised the execution of prisoners who were approved for death in the gas chamber.

Though there was an outcry from religious leaders when the program was first discovered, the Nazis realized that the lack of a large public response to this program, in which Germans were killed, meant that in all likelihood the outcry over Jews being killed in faraway camps would be virtually non-existent. They were right.

At the height of their power, the Nazis had concentration camps all over Europe – hundreds of them. Many of these housed Jews temporarily until they could be sent to the extermination camps or worked to death. Other prisoners included Russian POWs, Roma and Sinti people (also known as gypsies), homosexuals, criminals, political prisoners, and others such as the Jehovah's Witnesses, who refused to give in or did not fit into Nazi ideology.

Hundreds of thousands of men, women, and children died in the concentration camps – shootings, beatings, hanging, torture, disease, hunger were common causes of death. As horrible as these places were and sound at the current time, their primary purpose was incarceration and forced labor, not extermination. This concept came along a lot later when they realized that they did not have enough guards to supervise forced labor.

The first extermination camp was set up at Belzec, in the far east of Poland, in December 1941. Here, small gas chambers were built, which used carbon monoxide pumped into them from a large running engine. Victims were driven by whips, rifle butts, bayonets, and dogs down a fenced corridor and into the gas chambers. At first, cadavers belonging to victims were buried in mass graves, but the escape of gas from the bodies, and their emergence from the shallow graves, caused crematoria to be built in 1942. An estimated 350,000 to 500,000 victims were killed at Belzec. Later, in the spring and summer of 1942, two other camps in other parts of Poland, Sobibor, and Treblinka, were built and operated on the Belzec model. An estimated 250,000 victims died at Sobibor before a revolt caused the installation to be closed. Another 700,000 to 850,000 people were murdered at Treblinka.

Almost at the same time, a facility was built, or rather modified, near Chelmno to the northwest of Warsaw. Here, at a manor farm, Jews were led from a basement where they disrobed and were told they were going to be deloused and shipped to labor camps further east. Undressed, they were made to get into the back of a large truck, which was hermetically sealed, and whose exhaust pipes were fed back into the back of the vehicle. It then traveled four miles down a road to already dug burial pits. In 15-20 minutes, the victims were dead or comatose, and were dumped into the pits by other prisoners, who then washed out the van for its return journey for more victims.

Rudolf Höss, who had commanded the notorious concentration camps of Dachau and Sachsenhausen in the 1930s, was earmarked to become the commander of Auschwitz. He had been to personally visit SS leader Heinrich Himmler, who told him that the organized "Final Solution to the Jewish Problem" had been ordered by the Fuhrer, and that the camp at Oswiecim, Poland was to be expanded for this purpose. Höss was to oversee the building of said camp and extermination facilities.

Höss toured the other extermination facilities and observed the extermination process there. A man with a strict sense of order and professionalism, Höss was determined that his camp would be both more efficient and more "humane." You will read his disturbing testament of how "humane" his camp actually was in Chapter Three.

Chapter 5: Witold Pilecki and Auschwitz I

The first camp in the area, which came to be known as "Auschwitz I" in coming years, is today a museum and memorial. If one was totally ignorant of history, and walked through the area, one might think it had been an old military barracks, or perhaps even dormitories. To those who are well versed in history, it obviously was not. In its early years, (1940-1941), Auschwitz developed a reputation for brutality and death. This was *before* the building of Auschwitz II Birkenau – the extermination center.

Ceaseless brutality accompanied all who walked through the gates of Auschwitz I, with the infamous slogan of the concentration camps: "Arbeit Macht Frei" ("Work Sets You Free").

In the years 1939-45, men and women all over the world who loved freedom gave of themselves, all too often, eventually paying the ultimate price. Our history books are filled with the accounts of brave soldiers on the battlefields, at sea and in the skies. There are the stories of Resistance fighters risking all behind enemy lines, and men and women risking their lives and the lives of their families by rescuing Jews and others who were being hunted by the Nazis. There are undoubtedly countless others we shall never know about, and whose names are lost to history.

Most educated people today, when asked where the last place on Earth they would want to be sent to if time travel existed, would say "Auschwitz." Yet, there was a man who *volunteered* to go there and report to Poland and the world what was happening there. Seventy years after the war, people outside of Poland are only just beginning to learn of the incredible bravery of Polish Captain Witold Pilecki.

Pilecki, an intensely patriotic Pole, was also unbelievably brave and audacious. A co-founder of the underground Polish Secret Army ("Tajna Armia Polska" or "TAP," which would later become the "ZWZ" or "Związek Walki Zbrojnej," or "Union (Association) for Armed Struggle," and then the "AK" "Armie Krajowa"), Pilecki was disturbed by reports coming to him about the German camp at Oswiecim where, among others, arrested members of the TAP were being detained.

Pilecki developed a plan which would allow him to witness first-hand what was happening behind the wire in Auschwitz. He would allow himself to be captured. Via the Polish underground inside and outside the camp, Pilecki would get information on the camp out to the ZWZ/AK, which in turn relayed it to the Polish government in exile. This was done, in part, by relaying messages through released and escaped inmates. "Auschwitz I" was a "punishment" camp, not an extermination facility, fatal though it often was.

Another method was the paying of Polish civilians to relay information. This information, and information culled from the accounts of Polish resistance members like Jan Karski and other sources, would provide the basis of the pamphlet "Mass Extermination of Jews in Occupied Poland," which was published during the war by the Polish Government in Exile. Two months after his escape from Auschwitz in April of 1943, Pilecki would write a brief eleven-page outline of what he knew of Auschwitz. A one hundred page account of his experience in the camp followed not long after. After the war, he would write a much longer report for the Polish government, which not only described the camp itself and his experience there both as a prisoner and as one of the main organizers of an underground within the camp, but also would elaborate on conditions in the camp, the increasing ferocity of the treatment of Jews there, and the eventual extermination program at Birkenau.

As a Pole born in Tsarist Russia in 1901, Pilecki grew up with the experience of generations of Poles before him – with no Polish homeland. Divided by Prussia, Austria-Hungary, and Russia in various ways since 1772, by 1901, the Poles had been subject to the whims and laws of foreign rulers for one hundred and twenty nine years. This was to continue for another seventeen, for in 1918, Poland regained its independence with the fall of Tsarist Russia, and the defeat of Germany and Austria-Hungary. Having moved from Russia to Wilno (present day Vilnius, capital of Lithuania), Pilecki in the period 1918-21 took part in the Polish-Soviet war both as a regular and as an anti-Bolshevik, anti-Russian partisan, being twice decorated for valor. At the end of the war, Pilecki became a non-commissioned officer in the new Polish army, and five years later was commissioned a lieutenant in the Polish Army reserve. During this period, in addition to continuing his education, he presided over the family property, and more importantly became involved in the Polish paramilitary National Security Association where he was recognized as a natural leader.

By the time of Germany's invasion in 1939, Pilecki was a well-trained and much respected officer. Fighting in turn the Germans and the Soviets, Pilecki's division was destroyed fighting in the east on September 22nd, 1939, with the survivors surrendering to the Soviets, escaping to Hungary or, like Pilecki, going underground. It was in Warsaw in November of 1939 that Pilecki and two other Polish patriots, army Major Jan Wlodarkiewicz (1900-42) and World War I veteran Wladyslaw Surmacki (1888-1942), formed the Polish Secret Army.

Traveling under the identity of "Tomasz Serafinski," Pilecki walked into a German round up of Poles, and along with two thousand other people was taken to an army barracks where they were repeatedly beaten with truncheons, or thick sticks. They were kept there for two days, and already Pilecki noticed a proclivity toward "crowd psychology" on the part of the other Poles who were kept there with him. This "crowd psychology" was to become recognized as a feature of many Holocaust accounts in future years.

Two days later, Pilecki was crammed into a train bound for Auschwitz. This journey lasted for twenty four hours, and was marked by all of the characteristics of the train journeys of the Jews that became well known many years after the war was over – overcrowding and lack of hygiene, water, and food. Arriving at Auschwitz, Pilecki wrote one of the first descriptions of what life there was like. *"I consider this place in my story to be the moment when I bade farewell to everything I had hitherto know on this earth and entered into something seemingly no longer of it."* Later accounts by survivors, like that of Primo Levi, described Auschwitz in the same way: *"Instead, the arrival in the Lager was indeed a shock because of the surprise it entailed. The world into which one was precipitated was terrible, yes, but also indecipherable . . ."*

The first indication that what he had entered into did not resemble any prison camp that he had ever heard of was when one man from Pilecki's group was ordered to "escape," and run towards the side of the road. The man was then gunned down. Immediately afterward, ten other inmates were chosen at random and machine-gunned on the road as "collective responsibility" for the "escape." The SS guards laughed and joked at their atrocity. Throughout his three-year imprisonment in Auschwitz, Pilecki again and again dodged death. It was sometimes by the sheerest chance, like in the situation above, sometimes because of his resourcefulness, and many times through the kindness or favor of others.

Pilecki also learned, and was again one of the first to report, on the Nazi use of prisoners to do much of their dirty work. In two descriptive accounts (among many), Pilecki describes the sadism of many of the camps' "capos" (overseers), beginning with "Bloody Alois": "So we were sent off into Block 17A into the care of "Alois," later to become known as "Bloody Alois." He was a

German, a communist with a red "winkel". The colored triangular marking sewn onto the chest of prisoners' uniforms, each color denoting the category of prisoner. There were five colors of "winkel": red for communists, black for "asocial" (including people refusing to work, draft-dodgers, pacifists, among others), green – criminals, violet – Jehovah's Witnesses, and pink – homosexuals. Jews wore the Star of David. Alois was a degenerate who had already spent about six years in the camps, he beat tormented and tortured, with several corpses to his personal account every day.

For the slightest infraction, punishment was meted out. After holding a card with his prison number in his hand, rather than in his teeth as instructed, Pilecki had two teeth knocked out by a capo. "I was hit on the chin with a heavy club. I spat out two teeth. I bled a little... par for the course." Pilecki was to learn that this type of punishment was light in comparison to other forms of it in the camp. Soon after, he was subject to special punishments like "gymnastics," that the capos would inflict during roll call. "Gymnastics" consisted of strenuous calisthenics – done for hours. Inmates would drop like flies. Only those in shape like Pilecki due to his military service, or from physical labor on the outside, or those smart enough to know when to surreptitiously take a breather, like when the capos were beating another man to death, survived. Pilecki's description of "gymnastics" is almost identical to the later version of the same in the pamphlet, "Camp of Death," released in 1942 in Polish, and 1944 in English.

Though many of the capos were sadists themselves, the fact of the matter is that they were encouraged in their sadism by the SS staff of the camp, and these SS frequently indulged their own sadistic side. Pilecki mentions quite a few of them by name, and was meticulous in his recording of their names, their ranks, and their acts of sadism. Three examples out of an almost countless account of sadism in Pilecki's report will suffice here. There was "Pearlie," the nickname of a security man who had trained his dog to attack weak inmates, tear their genitals from them, and kill them. There was SS Obersturmfuehrer, (First Lieutenant) Gerhard Palitzsch, who scared even the SS ranks in the camp with his behaviour and zealousness, and who sometimes used a type of spring bolt used to kill cattle to murder human beings. Eventually, Palitzisch was convicted by the SS of theft, graft, and sexual misconduct, sent to a punishment battalion, and killed in action in 1945. SS Hauptsturmfuehrer (Captain) Fritz Seidler flogged inmates to death; frequently making them do calisthenics between strokes. Seidler also caused inmates to die of exposure by holding hours long roll calls in freezing winter weather.

Part of the roll-call area and the execution wall at Auschwitz I

All of this and more were reported by Pilecki in his extraordinarily detailed account. He described how to survive in the camp – to not go it alone, to secure a job indoors, and how to get extra food and medical care, among other things. It is important to remember that Pilecki was in Auschwitz I, the original camp, and while certainly hell on Earth, was not the extermination facility that was Auschwitz II – Birkenau.

Pilecki's mission was two-fold. He would report on conditions in the camp, and he would organize an underground and resistance movement in the camp. In his final report in 1945, Pilecki enumerated (in code) one hundred and eighty-four members of the Polish underground (the "Union of Military Organization," the

"ZOW," or Związek Organizacji Wojskowej) in the camp. Pilecki served as a conduit and peacemaker between underground groups of various political stripes, and helped to coordinate the placement of underground members in certain jobs. This was a task that Pilecki was well aware might cost another inmate his life, as someone else not in the underground must be either removed from the work or prevented from getting it. He also prepared them for the uprising which Pilecki hoped might either inspire a break-out from the camp, or perhaps an airborne (parachute) assault of the facility by the Allies.

Throughout the period 1940-42, Pilecki struggled to survive. He faced death every day, and was always in danger of being randomly chosen for a fatal beating or execution at the whim of a capo or SS man. As time went by however, Pilecki became influential among the inmates, and had even recruited, to one extent or another, capos into his organization. While this put him at less risk than other prisoners, every moment of life in Auschwitz could have been his last. He survived pneumonia and other ailments with the help of fellow Pole, Dr. Wladyslaw Dering, who was also in the ZOW, a group of underground resistance movements.

In 1942, Pilecki noticed changes going on in the camp. To begin with, the Jewish inmates of Auschwitz I were to a large extent given better jobs. This in itself was unusual, for Jews were usually singled out for especially harsh treatment. As it turned out, and as Pilecki put in his report at the end of the war, this was a ruse. The Jews were given these jobs and "encouraged" (i.e. coerced) to write letters to their families that they were well and thriving in their new location. After a few months, Pilecki says "...the Jews were suddenly rounded up and quickly 'finished off.'" In 1940, Pilecki and others had built the crematorium in Auschwitz I. "We were building the crematorium for ourselves." It was clear from the start that Auschwitz was intended as a place of death, but the scale of killing could not, by Pilecki in 1940, be imagined. By 1942, it could be, and would become a reality.

In his report after the war, Pilecki called the year 1942 "the most dreadful." As we now know, 1942 marked the beginning of the most deadly period of the Holocaust, and Pilecki noted all the aspects of the extermination process in his reports to and for the outside authorities in the Polish underground. He noted that Jews from all over Europe were beginning to arrive at Birkenau. He described the process of the selection and the sorting of belongings. He devotes much time to the description of the "Canada" section of Birkenau, where the possessions of newly arrived Jews were sorted into their assigned groups.

He also speaks of "organization," the theft and collection of items from "Canada" and elsewhere in the camp that helped other inmates survive, guards to be bribed, and civilian Poles to be paid for black-market goods and information to and from the camp. Pilecki's account of the murder of Jews in the gas chambers and in a later part of the report Pilecki notes the gassing of gypsies, was used both in the Polish government pamphlet "Mass Extermination of the Jews in Occupied Poland" and in the pamphlet "Camp of Death," released in Polish in 1942, and in English in 1944. The English version came with a preface by a member of Parliament. The account was remarkably accurate and would have informed anyone who wished to know what was happening in Auschwitz: "Then, in hundreds, women and children separately from the men, they went off to huts which were supposedly showers, but were [actually] gas chambers. The outside windows were fakes and inside there was a wall. After the tight fitting doors were shut, mass murder was committed inside... This lasted several minutes... Then they ventilated: doors on the side away from the ramp were opened and Jewish kommandos carried out the still warm bodies on wheelbarrows and carts to the nearby crematoria where the corpses were quickly burnt... The camp was like a huge mill, turning living people into [bodies, and then] ashes."

Pilecki tells of the sexual and medical experiments done in Block 10 of the camp, their cruelty and lethality. Pilecki also describes some of the attempted and successful escapes, including the audacious theft of the camp commandant's car by four inmates, who successfully drove off in SS uniform to freedom. One of these inmates took Pilecki's initial report on Auschwitz to the Polish underground. For every escape, however, there were many unsuccessful attempts, and retribution. Those who could not, or would not escape often "went to the wires" (committing suicide by enmeshing themselves in the electric fence which surrounded the camp) or committed suicide in another way.

Pilecki was remarkably successful in organizing, and keeping secret, the members of the ZOW. Members were organized by block or barracks on military lines, and were given assignments in the case of the uprising which Pilecki hoped would come in conjunction with an effort to liberate the camp by the AK, or "Home Army." Pilecki repeatedly insisted in messages relayed to the AK that the resistance in the camp was ready for an uprising, had weapons and a plan, and was only waiting for a signal from the higher command on the outside to implement it. Pilecki was to be repeatedly disappointed, for no matter how hard he pled his case for an uprising/raid, he was refused. The grounds given were that the AK did not have the manpower to spare, and what they did have available was not enough to fight against the numbers of well-equipped German troops in the camp, not to mention being unable to hold the camp for any length of time against any kind of German counter-assault.

As successful as Pilecki and his organization were in aiding other members, getting information into and out of the camp, planning an uprising and securing supplies for it, it was only a matter of time (in a camp full of people desperate to survive and willing to trade information to the Germans in order to do so), before the Germans closed in on the members of the ZOW and its leadership, of which Pilecki was a very important part.

In March of 1943, Pilecki got word that the Germans planned a large transport of Polish prisoners to other camps. Many were already being taken. It was at this point that he and two of his compatriots in the ZOW decided to attempt an escape. On the night of April 26-27, 1943, Pilecki and his companions escaped from the camp. Despite being shot in the arm during a very close call with a German sentry on the road four days after his escape from the camp,

Pilecki and his friends made it to freedom. In 1940, Pilecki had entered the camp under the alias "Tomasz Serafinski." In 1943, his resting place after the escape was, completely by chance, the home of Tomasz Serafinski – who was also a member of the Polish resistance. Serafinski had used the same forger as Pilecki to obtain false papers in Warsaw, but he had had to leave before the papers were ready. It was those papers that Witold Pilecki obtained, and the identity of this very same Tomasz Serafinski he had assumed in the camp.

During his period of recovery at the Serafinski home, Pilecki wrote his first account of his experience in Auschwitz. It was also during this time that he actively re-joined the Polish resistance. Having made his way to Warsaw in August of 1943, Pilecki took part in the Warsaw Uprising of 1944, serving with bravery. He was captured when the uprising ended on October 2, 1943, and interned in two German prison camps, being liberated from the POW camp in Murnau, Germany, in 1945. After being re-assigned by the Polish Army, that was fighting with the Western Allies, to Italy to recover and be briefed about the situation in Poland under the Soviets, Pilecki wrote his final report on Auschwitz.

Sadly, the story of Witold Pilecki does not have a happy ending. Returning to Poland under the assumed name of "Roman Jezierski" in October of '45, Pilecki reunited with his family and gathered information for the non-communist Polish government in exile in the West. Pilecki and others reported on increased Soviet influence, the setting up of a communist puppet government in Warsaw, (though Stalin had promised free elections), the execution of many Polish patriots, and the deportation of hundreds of Poles to Siberia by the Russian secret police, the NKVD.

Some of the people that were deported and were being investigated by the Soviets and their Polish counterparts were former members of Pilecki's ZOW in Auschwitz. In May of 1947, Pilecki was arrested by the communist government of Poland and charged with, among other things, espionage and plotting to assassinate members of the Polish secret police. Tortured, (he told a family member during a visit that the treatment he received from the Polish secret police was "child's-play" compared to what he had received in Auschwitz) and put on trial in a sham proceeding, Pilecki was sentenced to death. He was executed on the 25th of May 1948. Today, nearly 70 years after his death, the incredibly brave Witold Pilecki is considered a Polish national hero. In the ancient Polish capital of Krakow, his bust stands next to that of Marie Curie and Pope John Paul II. A Street in the town of Oswiecim bears his name. The following are a 1939 photo of Captain Pilecki and his Auschwitz prisoner photo in 1941.

Chapter 6: Dina Babbitt – Art in the Ruins

Dina Babbitt's survival story is unique in many ways. Interned at Auschwitz in 1943, Dina arrived with her mother. Her escape from the horror of the place was to create simple drawings. Another prisoner, having noticed her talent, asked her if she'd be willing to paint a mural in the prison to give the children there some hope. But someone very powerful had noticed her talent, also.

Dr. Josef Mengele was deeply dissatisfied with the ability of photography to convincingly portray the righteousness of Nazi theories of racial supremacy. He explained to Dina that he wanted her to paint representations of imprisoned Romani people, ordering that she make their skin sufficiently dark. Dina agreed to create the works on the condition that her mother's life be spared.

Mengele said he needed her mother's camp identification number (tattooed on the arms of all prisoners). Dina didn't know this and so Mengele sent for Dina's mother to come. The numbers of the two women were recorded and added to a list of prisoners who were to be spared.

Dina had been an art student until the Nazi invasion of her country, Czechoslovakia. Their arrival had forced her to abandon her studies, due to the fact she was Jewish.

Dina later said: "Being so excruciatingly hungry all the time, with no hope of being sated was just more pain for us. While I was painting, I was able to lift myself out of the hunger and horror of life in the camp."

Mengele gave Dina the supplies she needed to paint her Gypsy subjects – paints and a pad of art paper and two chairs. One, she was instructed to employ as an easel and the other was for those she would paint.

A young woman named Celine was selected for Dina to capture in watercolors. Dina remembers that "*Celine had recently lost a child. With the lack of food in the camp, it hadn't been possible for her to nurse the infant and the baby had died of starvation. I was fed on decent soup and bread while painting and was able to give this to Celine. I took my time painting her. The longer she was with me, the longer it was assured she would stay alive and at least eat a little better than others in the camp."*

One day, while Mengele was inspecting her work, he noted that Dina hadn't signed it. He pointed out to Dina that all her paintings should bear her signature.

She asked him, *"Is that my name you mean?"* She was unsure as to whether Mengele was asking her to sign with the number tattooed on her arm. He responded that she should sign with her name.

And so it is that each of the seven surviving works Dina created in Auschwitz bears her first name. After the war, it was Dina's belief that all her paintings had been lost in the midst of the chaos and confusion that marked the war's end.

But like Dina, the art she'd produced at Auschwitz survived. These might never have been identified, if Mengele hadn't pointed out that Dina hadn't signed them and ordered that she do so. This detail serves as a rather odd footnote to the Angel of Death's otherwise notorious legacy.

It was eventually discovered that Dina's artwork was in the Auschwitz Museum. The paintings had originally been found by a fellow prisoner and kept safe, but later given to area people who had sheltered a Hungarian child, in appreciation of their kindness. That same child was to sell the works to the Auschwitz Museum, in 1963. Not until six years later was the Museum's curator able to discern who had created them. It was then that the search for Dina began.

In 1973, the museum invited Dina to come to Auschwitz in order to identify the works.

Dina was overjoyed to discover that the art she'd created while interned at Auschwitz still existed. She hadn't believed she'd ever see the paintings again.

But the discovery was bittersweet. The Museum refused to permit her to take the paintings home with her to the United States, where she had started her life again, after the war.

Sadly, Dina would spend the rest of her life attempting to recover her paintings. The Museum sympathized with Dina's need to have these paintings with her. Administrators there understood that they were an emotional and poignant memorial of Dina's internment at Auschwitz. But it was never to be. The argument of administrators was that these works were of enormous historical significance; that they needed to be on public display for the sake of educating future generations about the Holocaust. Regardless of the fact that Dina was a survivor of the camps and had created the art, public patrimony won the day and Dina, once again, lost what she had created in the crucible of war and internment.

On returning home, Dina made a formal request to the Museum to return her paintings, which was rejected. But she didn't stop there.

Prior to her death in 2009, Dina's struggle to get back the art she'd created in Auschwitz garnered a great deal of interest in the USA. There was even involvement by US Senators like Barbara Boxer and Jesse Helms.

A House resolution written by Representative Shelley Berkley supported Dina's claim. A similar resolution was presented in the Senate by Boxer and Helms. Both resolutions were unanimously passed in the two government Houses in 2003. Support for her position was received from a wide variety of people, some of them very prominent. But Dina was to die short of the goal of reclaiming the paintings.

Of the Museum's intractability on the issue, her daughter said:

"This feels like she's been incarcerated again. The importance of those paintings in my mother's life is inestimable. She feels that a part of herself is being interned."

Dina passed away in 2009. As she fought for her life in Auschwitz, she fought for the return of the works she'd been commissioned to paint by Dr. Josef Mengele. Her enduring legacy to the world is both the paintings which continue to be displayed at the Auschwitz Museum, and the poignancy of her struggle to reclaim them.

Chapter 7: David Mermelstein – A Narrow Escape

David Mermelstein was 15 years old in 1944, the year he and his family were deported to Auschwitz-Birkenau. With his entire family, David arrived at the camp, completely ignorant of its purpose.

"We had no concept of what this place was, or that it even existed," he said during a recent speaking engagement. *"They told us were being sent to Auschwitz to work. Beyond that, we had no idea what to expect."*

David and his family were part of a group of about 100 other deportees. Their transport was small and cramped to the breaking point. When they entered the camp and were herded off the wagon they were in, they were met by Josef Mengele. Now internationally known as the Angel of Death, this monstrous person is remembered for his sadism and medical experiments on those interned at Auschwitz.

Auschwitz's infamous selection of those who would be gassed immediately began shortly after David's arrival. Ruthlessly, the Nazis began to sort the newly-arrived prisoners.

"I watched as my entire family was selected and send to the left hand side. This meant, I now know, that they were to be exterminated in the gas chambers," he relates. *"An inmate working as a supervisor for the Nazis came near me and quietly said I should tell the guards I was older than I actually was. He said to convince them of this by not slouching. He also suggested I induce a flush in my cheeks by pinching them."*

David survived selection using the feet of his older brothers to stand on, rendering him taller than he was, as he gave his age to the guards. With his brothers, David was thus told to move to the right. All three of the boys would perform forced labor in the camp. David remembers what happened next:

"We were pushed into another area. Here we were ordered to strip nude, save for our shoes. We were then instructed to put on the camp uniform, the iconic tunic, trousers and cap of the concentration camps."

David and his brothers asked one of the guards about the whereabouts of their parents and grandparents, who had been with several other members of their family. The guard, of course, responded with no regard for the feelings of the boys. Instructing David and the other new arrivals to look out the door, he said:

"Do you see the smoke in the sky? This is what's left of them now."

In the days to come, David would learn the truth about where he and his family had been sent. He would come to intimately know the brutal reality of the situation he and his brothers were in.

He recalls the moment he first understood what the meaning of the smoke in the sky over Auschwitz was:

"Some inmates were calling to the new prisoners across one of the fences that separated the different sections of the camp. As the new arrivals approached to respond, they reached out to touch the fence, only to be electrocuted where they stood."

Through the years of his imprisonment, David learned how to evade death. He labored through illness in order that it would go undetected by the guards. He knew that if he let on he was sick, he'd be gassed in short order. Those who couldn't work, he came to know, were immediately dispensed with.

It was the fall of 1944 when David was sent on a death march to the Emaze camp, in Austria. There he was assigned to work on the wagons that transported coal around the camp. He began to take lumps of coal whenever he could and eat them. Food was becoming increasingly scarce, and by doing this, David was able to survive another day. Desperation compelled him and he did not hesitate even to eat coal, in order to survive.

To add to David's misery, his hand was seriously injured while working on the coal wagons, necessitating his removal from the work party. Unable to continue performing forced labor, he was put in hospital. There he learned exactly what purpose this purported medical facility served. It was the last station on the way to the camp's terminus – the gas chambers and the smoke in the sky.

"Talking to others prisoners in the hospital, I believed I had no more than 19 days to live before meeting my fate," David explains. He'd deduced this by making note of the comings and goings of other prisoners. He would count the days from the arrival of each to the day on which they were removed, never to return.

"One day, shortly before my presumed last day, I woke up to see that there were no guards. Some of us got out of bed to see what was going on. I was too weak to get out of bed at this point and so I waited. When the others returned, they were shouting that our former captors had apparently fled, leaving the gates of Auschwitz wide open."

At this point, David was desperately weak with abuse and overwork he'd been subjected to. He could no longer walk, so he crawled to make it out of the camp. This painful liberation took him no less than three hours. He remembers his realization that the camp had been liberated:

"Once I'd made it out through the gates, crawling painfully on my belly, I saw an American flag, mounted on a military vehicle. I realized that the Allies had taken the camp, sending the Germans running. There were facilities being set up to tend to the many sick in the camp and to prepare food for us."

The Allied doctors discovered that David had been lucky to see the liberation of Auschwitz arrive, at all. On weighing him, it was discovered he weighed under 45 pounds. As the Allies, tended to him, David began to regain his strength, but was unable to walk for a month and a half after the liberation of the camp. A slow, but deliberate return to normal health under the care of the Allies followed.

Today, David Mermelstein is 86 years old and lives in Miami, home to a large community of survivors of the camps. He gives his time to efforts to keep the memory of the Holocaust and its lessons for humanity alive, that people might never forget.

The young man who crawled through the open gates of Auschwitz to life and freedom, now shares his knowledge with people the same age he was then.

Chapter 8: Gena Turgel – From the Jaws of Death, to the Arms of Love

There's a bittersweet quality to the story of Gena Turgel. Today, Gena is 90 years old and a great-grandmother, but she was only a girl when Hitler's armies consumed Europe. Gena relates that she likes to wear a lot of perfume, because *"the stench of that place and the others is still with me. I can't bear it and so I drown it in perfume"*.

Gena was 16 when, in 1939, the Germans began to bomb her hometown of Krakow, Poland. What followed was the systematic marginalization of the Jewish people. At the time, the family had been trying to find a way out of Hitler's Europe, fearing the worst. With family in Chicago, they'd hoped it would be possible to leave for America. Instead, they found themselves sealed in a ghetto. Established in 1941, thousands of Polish Jews found themselves in what amounted to holding areas for those destined for the concentration camps. These were dissolved and those living in them shipped out to area camps. When the moment came, later that same year, Gena's family was separated, but she, her sister and mother remained together.

In all, Gena Turgel was to be held in three separate camps. The first of these was Plaszov, where she and her sister, Miriam, shared a bunk.

"I always slept on the right, with Miriam on the left. It's as though I can still sense her with me. Sometimes I have the strangest sensation on the arm she would lay against at night, as though I can't stay warm without her," Dena relates.

Shortly after the arrival of the two sisters at Pleszov, Mirian was killed by guards when caught smuggling food.

Their mother was forced to carry wood to the incinerators. Gena imagines how she must have felt:

"Imagine that you've been ripped from your home and separated from members of your family. You're put in prison for no reason at all, save the megalomania of some dictator. Then they murder your daughter and force you to carry wood to the place where they plan to burn her body."

After almost three years in Pleszov, Gena and many others were made to march to the Auschwitz camp. It was there that Gena experienced some of the worst abuses of the war. Subjected to the gruesome experiments of Dr. Mengele, she somehow lived on.

But the cruelty of the Angel of Death was not all Gena was to survive at Auschwitz.

In 1944, when she was 21 years old, Gena and her mother were taken under guard to the camp's extermination facilities. There they were ordered to remove their clothing and stay in the room they'd been put in until further notice.

"We were terrified and naked in this cold room, not knowing what was going to happen next. Suddenly the water came on. We hadn't had any water for quite some time, so the feeling of it on our skin was the most joyous sensation," Gena remembers.

"Afterward, we dressed and went back outside. No one was there to stop us. There were some women prisoners there and they were astounded to see us alive. They were overcome with joy and began shouting at us.

When I asked them what the fuss was about, they told me that mother and I had been in the gas chamber. I opened my mouth, but nothing came out. My throat became so tight and dry with the shock of it, I couldn't even swallow.

Sometimes I can't believe I'm still alive to tell this tale. I don't really understand why I am," Gena says.

It was only a short while later than Gena, with her mother, was again transferred. This time, she was sent to Buchenwald. With the Allies closing in and Germany becoming increasingly aware it was about to lose the war, the Nazis were panicked. Gena and her mother were moved again in short order. This would be their final destination before the end of the war. They were marched with other inmates to Bergen-Belsen, in the middle of winter, in sub zero temperatures.

Then, on April 15, 1945, Bergen-Belsen was liberated by the Allies. Dena and her mother, among 60,000 other prisoners, were finally free.

One of the first soldiers to enter the camp was Norman Turgel. Serving with the British Army, he was to round up the top tier of the camp's SS officers. What he saw was something he'd never forget. The ground was littered with the corpses of prisoners – more than 13,000 of them. Those prisoners still living were on the point of death themselves, many ill with diseases like typhus.

But there was one prisoner Norman couldn't forget either – Dena.

The young officer was so taken with Dena that he was to invite her to eat with him in the officer's mess and demand that she marry him. She was taken aback at his resolve:

"He wouldn't take no for an answer. Rather pigheaded, actually."

The two were in love and while she was deeply scarred by what had happened to her under Nazi occupation and in the camps, Dena agreed to marry him. Six months after meeting, Dena married Norman in a synagogue the Nazis had used to house livestock. Her gown was fashioned of a parachute used by the British Army.

Today Dena lives in England. Norman has passed on. She dedicates her time to family and promoting public awareness about the Holocaust. In 2000, she became an MBE for her work with the Holocaust Foundation, educating children about genocide in the hope of eradicating it.

Dena Turgel continues to live with the horrors of Auschwitz as well as the two other camps she survived. Always at the edge of her consciousness, the images, smells and memories lurk.

She says *"I do my best to keep myself occupied. There is only so much of one's life one can spend in the past, because life is to be lived as well as one can, in this moment. Life is a tremendous gift. If one is grateful, it's impossible not to live it fully. It's a miracle that I'm here and I mean to honor that for all the time I have left."*

Chapter 9: The Great Escape

Kazimierz Piechowsky spent his childhood in the Polish town of Tczew. There he enjoyed an idyllic early life. His family was of modest, but comfortable means. At the age of ten, Kazimierz became a boy scout. This one act would become one of the most important of his life, as it turns out.

When he was only 19 years old, in 1939, the Germans invaded Poland. The Nazis were opposed to the boy scouts. Organized groups that were not directly overseen by them were always seen as threats to their domination. Because of this, they systematically targeted members, rounding them up and killing them. Some of these were Kazimierz's friends. He remembers fearing he would be next:

"When it became clear what was happening, I decided then and there that I would not be the next scout murdered. I ran away."

Kazimierz fled to Poland's Hungarian frontier. Some of his fellows had already attempted the same, in order to join with the independent Polish forces fighting there. But at the border, the Nazis arrested him. He was moved between a number of facilities and finally, shipped to Auschwitz.

Because he was on one of the first trains to ever be sent to the infamous death camp, it was Kazimierz's dubious distinction to be put to work in its construction. With the continuing mass apprehensions taking place at the time, Auschwitz simply could not accommodate all the people who were being detained there. Kazimierz remembers the endless labor:

"The norm was twelve or even fifteen hours, each day. What we were working on was the apparatus of extermination; the death camp. This is why the Nazis were in such a tremendous rush. They had set in motion the wheels of the Final Solution."

The shock of detention in this notorious camp was immediate, but when it wore off, the depraved conditions of the place and the treatment prisoners were subjected to, took their toll. In this overcrowded facility, the SS guards would do anything they felt necessary to contain the possibility of any unrest in the ranks of the inmates. Until the middle of 1941, guards beating inmates to death was routine. Not only did these summary murders send the message that no rebellion was to be tolerated, but the Nazis wanted to free up much needed space, so the practice served their purposes well. It further served the guards by reducing the number of prisoners for which they were responsible.

But it was so much more than the threat of death at Auschwitz that was beyond the limit of most people's imaginations. It was the lack of adequate food and the endless hard labor:

"We were never given enough to eat and what they gave us to eat with was only one spoon and bowl. In these we were also expected to empty our bladders, at night. Losing the spoon meant eating from the bowl with your hands, placing your mouth on the receptacle into which you'd urinated in the night. Losing your bowl meant you would get nothing to go in it; nothing to eat," Kazimierz explains.

Boredom was another enemy at the camps. The boredom of the guards left in the hellish, sadistic killing field of Auschwitz was nothing short of deadly. To amuse themselves, they would concoct entertainments for themselves that involved shooting inmates in the back. For the sake of order, these guards would sometimes be upbraided by superiors, but punishment received would be more like a reward. The guards would simply claim the prisoners they'd shot had been attempting an escape. Their superiors, pleased with such effective and efficient action, would provide the days off the guards had been angling for in the first place.

For some of his time at Auschwitz, Kazimierz was put to work removing the bodies of the dead. He explains the job in grisly terms:

"There was a wall between two of the blocks in the camp. This was where prisoners would be shot. They would be told to stand with their faces to the wall and then, shot dead. Every day, there would be piles of corpses to be taken away to be burned. These would always be naked, as they had already been stripped of their uniforms, after death. Conditions were such that prisoners would often scavenge whatever they could from the dead. The philosophy was that they no longer needed whatever it was the living took from them.

Two of us would haul the corpses to a wagon and then take the wagon to the crematorium. Anywhere from twenty to over one hundred corpses we disposed of, each day. Women and children were always among them."

Something the Nazis didn't count on was that the spirit of the boy scouts, despite their best efforts to annihilate them, would live on in the camps. At Auschwitz, an informal network of resistance grew up among former members detained there and Kazimierz was part of it:

"I'd been more or less resigned to my fate in this hell until the day I was told that the name of a friend was on a list of those to be exterminated. Because of the network in the camp, I found this out. Because some of the scouts could speak German, they would be given posts in areas of the camp where they had access to a variety of information. This is how I found out about my friend's name being on the list. It was at this time I began contemplating breaking out of Auschwitz," he remembers.

Another member of the network, Eugenius Bendera, had given Kazimierz the dreadful news about his friend. A skilled motor mechanic, he told Kazimierz he could also get his hands on a car.

Because the men were in a heavily fortified section of the camp, they would need to drive out of the camp straight through its main entrance and then, through the barricade beyond that.

At this time, Kazimierz was working in an area in which Nazi uniforms and a variety of ammunition was stored. While there, he began thinking about how he could help his friend and escape, at the same time. All that was holding him back were Nazi threats about what would happen in the event of such a bold action:

"The Nazis were always pontificating about what would happen to us if we ever tried to get out of the camp. One day, one of them launched into this favored rant. The occasion was the arrival of a transport filled with new prisoners. He said that for every escaping prisoner, ten would be shot. I was afraid of what would happen to those left behind, should I escape."

In order to protect other members of their work party from Nazi retribution, Kazimierz and his fellow conspirators created a new group, completely false, to fool the Germans. In this group were four men, including another former boy scout and a priest…and Kazimierz's friend, marked for death.

In late June of 1942, the group met in a half-completed building to go over their plans. This was a half day off for the guards and the group knew that a number of areas would be left unguarded for a brief period of time.

"It was terrifying, but we all knew that if we failed, my friend would be shot and us with him. All of us agreed that failure was not an option, but that in the event of capture, we would commit suicide before going back inside. We were on tenterhooks with the tension of it all. Somehow, though, I knew we'd make it," Kazimierz remembers.

When the time came, the four made their way toward the main entrance of the camp, taking a large garbage bin with them. When the guard asked what they were doing, Kazimierz told him they were on garbage detail. Not bothering to check whether this was true or not, the guard let them through the gate. The four men made their way to the building where the uniforms and ammunition were kept. Kazimierz recalls swallowing his fear:

"My mind was entirely on the job at hand and not getting caught. Holding ourselves together and calling on all our faculties was my complete focus."

Kazimierz had deliberately fiddled with the locks in the building at work that day. They were able to gain entry to the stores in this way. Once in the stores section of the building, the four men went to the second floor, where the uniforms were located. Breaking into the room Kazimierz knew they were located, the four donned the uniform of the Third Reich. Eugenius Bendera had copied a key for the garage and one for a car kept there, in the course of his work in the mechanic shop. When all were dressed, they retrieved the vehicle and climbed inside.

For the escape, Eugenius had selected the fastest car in possession of the Nazis at the camp. They wanted a car capable of reaching Berlin in a matter of hours and also, to outrun the Nazis in the event they were detected.

As the escapees drove through the camp, SS officers greeted them with the Nazi salute, which they obligingly returned. Now moving toward the gate, none of them knew whether there would be any requirement for official permission to remove the car from the premises. They had no idea what to expect. As Kazimierz recounts:

"We all believed in my ability to mimic an SS man to perfection. We had to believe that we would pass without incident, or we never could have done it."

The moment of truth was rapidly approaching as the car moved closer and closer to the entrance of Auschwitz, notoriously bearing the legend: *"Arbeid macht frei"* (Work will set your free.

No move was made by the guard to open the gate. As the car moved nearer to its objective, the guard simply stood there. Finally, when they group was only 20 metres from the closed main entrance of Auschwitz, all four men were frozen with terror. Kazimierz describes the tension in the vehicle, as it neared the gate:

"You could have cut the fear with a knife. Eugenius had stopped the car, unsure as to what he should do. I began to yell, at the top of lungs in typical SS fashion, ordering the driver to move and the guard at the gate to hurry up and open the damned thing. That was all it took. The main gate of Auschwitz flew open and we drove through it."

In that moment, all Nazi delusions about their presumed superiority evaporated for at least some of their officers, as they questioned how it was that this band of "deficients" could escape. How they could do it with the Commandant's own vehicle, while dressed in full German uniform drove them to distraction. They were absolutely furious.

But there was a heavy price to pay for this bold act. The parents of one of the escapees were arrested, to die later in the camp the four men had just escaped from. Their audacity also led to the Auschwitz protocol of tattooing all prisoners with a unique number. In a fit of petty retribution for this slight against the Third Reich, the Nazis lashed out at whoever they could to make clear that the Great Escape would not be happening again any time soon.

Since his time in Auschwitz, Kazimierz has been plagued by memories and nightmares; demons he exorcises by traveling the world and writing. He has written two books about his experiences in the concentration camp complex of the Third Reich. His most fervent wish is that none of it is ever forgotten.

Once a boy scout, always a boy scout. It seems the Nazis were right to fear them.

Chapter 10: Birkenau

The post-war affidavit of Commandant Rudolf Höss reads like both a nightmare and an office memorandum, which makes it that much more horrifying...

Rudolf Höss born in 1900, joined the SS in 1933, and eventually commanded the massive extermination center of Auschwitz, whose name has come to symbolize humanity's ultimate descent into evil. This is his signed testimony at the Post-War trials of Major War Criminals held at Nuremberg burg.

1, RUDOLF FRANZ FERDINAND HOESS, being first duly sworn, depose and say as follows:

1. I am forty-six years old, and have been a member of the NSDAPI since 1922; a member of the SS since 1934; a member of the Waffen-SS since 1939. I was a member from 1 December 1934 of the SS Guard Unit, the so-called Deaths-head Formation (Totenkopfverbände).

2. I have been constantly associated with the administration of concentration camps since 1934, serving at Dachau until 1938; then as Adjutant in Sachsenhausen from 1938 to 1 May 1940, when I was appointed Commandant of Auschwitz. I commanded Auschwitz until 1 December, 1943, and estimate that at least 2,500,000 victims were executed and exterminated there by gassing and burning, and at least another half million succumbed to starvation and disease, making a total dead of about 3,000,000. This figure represents about 70% or 80% of all persons sent to Auschwitz as prisoners, the remainder having been selected and used for slave labor in the concentration camp industries. Included among the executed and burnt were approximately 20,000 Russian prisoners of war (previously screened out of Prisoner of War cages by the Gestapo) who were delivered at Auschwitz in Wehrmacht transports operated by regular Wehrmacht officers and men. The remainder of the total number of victims included about 100,000 German Jews, and great numbers of citizens (mostly Jewish) from Holland, France, Belgium, Poland, Hungary, Czechoslovakia, Greece, or other countries. We executed about 400,000 Hungarian Jews alone at Auschwitz in the summer of 1944.

4. Mass executions by gassing commenced during the summer 1941 and continued until fall 1944. I personally supervised executions at Auschwitz until the first of December 1943 and know by reason of my continued duties in the Inspectorate of Concentration Camps WVHA2 that these mass executions continued as stated above. All mass executions by gassing took place under the direct order, supervision and responsibility of RSHA. 31 received all orders for carrying out these mass executions directly from RSHA.

6. The "final solution" of the Jewish question meant the complete extermination of all Jews in Europe. I was ordered to establish extermination facilities at Auschwitz in June 1941. At that time there were already in the general government three other extermination camps; BELZEK, TREBLINKA and WOLZEK. These camps were under the Einsatzkommando of the Security Police and SD. I visited Treblinka to find out how they carried out their exterminations. The Camp Commandant at Treblinka told me that he had liquidated 80,000 in the course of one-half year. He was principally concerned with liquidating all the Jews from the Warsaw Ghetto. He used monoxide gas and I did not think that his methods were very efficient. So when I set up the extermination building at Auschwitz, I used Cyclon B, which was a crystallized Prussic Acid, which we dropped into the death chamber from a small opening. It took from 3 to 15 minutes to kill the people in the death chamber depending upon climatic conditions. We knew when the people were dead because their screaming stopped. We usually waited about one-half hour before we opened the doors and removed the bodies. After the bodies were removed our special commandos took off the rings and extracted the gold from the teeth of the corpses.

7. Another improvement we made over Treblinka was that we built our gas chambers to accommodate 2,000 people at one time, whereas at Treblinka their 10 gas chambers only accommodated 200 people each. The way we selected our victims was as follows: we had two SS doctors on duty at Auschwitz to examine

the incoming transports of prisoners. The prisoners would be marched by one of the doctors who would make spot decisions as they walked by. Those who were fit for work were sent into the Camp. Others were sent immediately to the extermination plants. Children of tender years were invariably exterminated since by reason of their youth they were unable to work. Still another improvement we made over Treblinka was that at Treblinka the victims almost always knew that they were to be exterminated and at Auschwitz we endeavoured to fool the victims into thinking that they were to go through a delousing process. Of course, frequently they realized our true intentions and we sometimes had riots and difficulties due to that fact. Very frequently women would hide their children under the clothes but of course when we found them we would send the children in to be exterminated. We were required to carry out these exterminations in secrecy but of course the foul and nauseating stench from the continuous burning of bodies permeated the entire area and all of the people living in the surrounding communities knew that exterminations were going on at Auschwitz.

8. We received from time to time special prisoners from the local Gestapo office. The SS doctors killed such prisoners by injections of benzine. Doctors had orders to write ordinary death certificates and could put down any reason at all for the cause of death.

9. From time to time we conducted medical experiments on women inmates, including sterilization and experiments relating to cancer. Most of the people who died under these experiments had been already condemned to death by the Gestapo.

10. Rudolf Mildner was the chief of the Gestapo at Kattowicz and as such was head of the political department at Auschwitz, which conducted third degree methods of interrogation from approximately March 1941 until September 1943. As such, he frequently sent prisoners to Auschwitz for incarceration or execution. He visited Auschwitz on several occasions. The Gestapo Court, the SS Standgericht, which tried person's accused of various crimes, such as escaping Prisoners of War, etc., frequently met within Auschwitz, and Mildner often

attended the trial of such persons, who usually were executed in Auschwitz following their sentence. I showed Mildner throughout the extermination plant at Auschwitz and he was directly interested in it since he had to send the Jews from his territory for execution at Auschwitz.

I understand English as it is written above. The above statements are true; this declaration is made by me voluntarily and without compulsion; after reading over the statement, I have signed and executed the same at Nurnberg, Germany on the fifth day of April 1946.

Rudolf Franz Ferdinand Höss, "Affidavit, 5 April 1946," in Trial of the Major War Criminals Before the International Tribunal, Nuremberg, 14 November 1945 1 October 1946 (Nuremberg: Secretariat of the International Military Tribunal, 1949), Doc. 3868-PS, vol. 33, 275 – 79.

Rudolf Höss in Allied captivity at war's end, before his death by hanging.

That was existence and death at Birkenau from its "humane" commander. What follows are accounts of those who survived the "humanity" of the SS, so that we might learn and remember.

Survivor Hugo Gryn, Summer 1994 – Arrival in Auschwitz-Birkenau:

I got out, and that was the point where my whole life was saved. There were these peculiar-looking people in striped uniforms. I made the assumption that they were inhabitants of the local lunatic asylum. They were moving up and down, their job was to clear the rains, but one of them, as he passed me, he's muttering in Yiddish, 'You're eighteen and you've got a trade, you're eighteen and you've got a trade.' And my father says to me, 'If they ask you anything, you're nineteen and you are a Tischler und Zimmermann – a joiner and carpenter. Gabriel, my brother, was eleven – extraordinarily lovely, a very, very bright boy; we came to the head of the line, they ask how old I am, I say nineteen.

"Betreibst du in Handwerk?" "Are you skilled in a trade?"

"Ja, ein Tischler und ein Zimmermann" "Yes, a joiner and a carpenter."

They don't even ask my brother and he is sent one way with my grandfather and grandmother, and my father and I another, my mother in roughly the same direction. My mother is not going to let my brother go without her, and the last I saw of her was her being pulled back roughly and sent in our direction, although the men and women were separated there. Later, in the barracks, I asked what happened about family reunions - you know: when are we going to meet the women and the others? How does it work? This man, who had been there who had been there for some time, said, "You'll never see them again."

I said "Why not?"

He says, "Well, by now they're dead."

"What do you mean 'they're dead?' Look, I'm so scared don't make bad jokes." Will you believe it, I didn't believe it, and I didn't believe what was happening there for at least twenty four hours."

In 1944, Italy was occupied by the Nazis after the fall of the Mussolini government. The Italians, who up to this point had been reluctant to hand over Italian Jews to the Germans, were forced to. This is an account of the experience of one of them. Ironically, in Italian, her last name "Tedeschi" is the Italian word for "German."

Giuliana Tedeschi, Auschwitz, May 1944. Punishment:

Shoved violently out of the block, I fell to my knees on the bare earth. Thinner than ever, in the white nightshirt that left arms and neck exposed, my curly hair cut short, I looked like an adolescent. Around me was the vastness of the night: I buried myself in it, I took refuge in it. The starry sky was close; it was a friend. So cold and so foreign by day when it was almost always covered by big storm clouds, tonight that Polish sky had something mysterious and familiar about it, something of the sky of my home country far away. With joy I recognized the Great Bear, as if it were an old family friend, then the polestar, Venus with its three stars in line, all the same. At that hour of the night the camp looked sinister, with its interminable rows of dark silent blocks, the barbed-wire boundary fence lit by powerful lamps all around, and the ghostly white path of the searchlight ruthlessly coming on and off as it hunted down your humiliated individuality in the general misery.

Inside the huts, huddled bodies vainly sought some rest after the daily toils, some respite from desperation. Everybody's sleep was disturbed, populated by ghosts; among the frequent cries and groans, the word 'mama' could be heard coming like some distressed plea from the lips of the young sleepers. In a silence and darkness deprived of the relaxation that night should bring, the stars seemed to belong to a different world, where our infinite misery was unknown. And in the abandon of the sleeping camp you saw that misery more clearly and sharply than during the gigantic struggle for existence that went on in the light of day. I had violent pains in one wrist and down one side where the kapo's club had beat me just a few minutes ago to remind me not to break the Lagerruhe, the strict silence that must be kept after eight in the evening. There would have been no point in trying to explain that I hadn't slept for three nights, that I was literally suffocating, crammed and crushed between eight other prisoners, that a Belgian was stealing my place, that... The ground was hard, and clods and pebbles pressed into my flesh. I clutched my arms to my breasts and shivered in that May night, frosty as an Italian night in February. Never before had I had such a strong feeling of being a grain of sand lost in the infinity of the universe. I was seized by dismay and desperation. In front of me the block windows reflected the light of a fire, and the same red flame flickered across a hundred other windows. The whole camp seemed to be on fire. That flame... I tried to find some way not to see it but couldn't.

High up, over the chimney of the crematorium, commanding the scene, it had reddened a corner of the sky. It burned night and day. I heard the confused sounds of people who had got off the train and were heading, unawares, to the doors of the mysterious building. I didn't dare turn around, that glow paralyzed me, and in my state of spiritual prostration an overwhelming desperation took hold of me. Something appalling had happened before my eyes, something which so far I had sought at all costs to avoid and which tormented me far more than the pain in my wrist and knees. I had been shaken to the core, my human dignity had been violated, violated by an abject being who knew nothing of me or the world. I threw myself face-down on the ground and wept and suffered terribly at the thought that I had a husband and children. I wanted to be alone, to be the only one who need think about my destiny. From a lookout post came the sound of an accordion accompanied by a grating male voice: the guard Posten, who watched over all this misery in the constant presence of that flame, had found a way to pass the time and relieve the boredom of his watch. Two delicate hands laid a smock on my shoulders, and a voice I didn't know muttered something. I recognized her in the glow from the flame: a Frenchwoman, quite old, who worked in the Schuhkommando, one of those dull creatures, without life or intelligence, who in normal circumstances barely manage to get by, and who in the camps seemed mad and moronic. I threw my arms around the neck of this companion in punishment, while to console me she whispered:

"Na et finir, mon petit, Na et finir; bientot"

Chapter 11: Miriam & Eva– The Twins Who Survived the Odds

Eva and Miriam were twin sisters and a part of a 6-member family that consisted of them, two elder sisters and their parents. This 6 member Jewish family lived in a tiny village that was situated in Romania. Being the only Jews in the entire area, they were pretty confident that the Germans wouldn't waste time and resources on them. Well, their confidence was in the wrong place and they were proved wrong.

The twins, Eva and Miriam were about 10 years old when the Germans came for them and their family. They were herded like cattle into a crowded car, one that was meant to transport farm animals, and were then taken to Simleul Silvanei. Then from there they were deported off to Auschwitz.

As soon as the family reached Auschwitz, the twins were separated from their family within the first half an hour that they were there. Their mother was attempting to shiled the twins when they realized that their father and their older sisters had disappeared. A man from the SS walked quickly past them shouting about them. When his eyes fell on the twins, he asked their mother if they were twins. When she hesitantly agreed, this guard dragged the girls away from their mother without another word. The twins and their mother screamed and struggled, but no one paid attention to them.

This moment would be the last that the twins ever saw their mother.

They were dragged to the children's barrack and left there. What they saw there made their blood freeze in their veins, but also strengthened their resolves.

Eva later said that the first time she went to use a latrine toward the end of the children's barracks, she saw children's corpses strewn about the ground. Noting that the image would stick with Eva forever, she made a pledge to herself, which was in her words, a *"vow to make sure that Miriam and I didn't end up on that filthy floor."*

Josep Mengele, often referred to as "*Uncle Mengele*" and "The Angel of Death", often conducted experiments on children as young as 5, injecting them with various chemicals, poisons and serums to see their effects on them.

There was a high demand for twins for various experiments and often one of the twins was experimented upon, while the other was used as a yardstick to measure the changes that took place. Children were often injected in the eye with chemicals in an attempt to change their eye color, surgeries were performed without any anesthesia, blood was transfused from one twin to the next, sex change operations were carried out and various organs and limbs were removed.

While Eva and Miriam lived there, a pair of Gypsy twins arrived at the child barracks. They had just been released from Mengele's laboratory, once they had been sewn back. The experiment conducted on them? Mengele tried to make Siamese twins by connecting the organs and blood vessels of the twins. The experiment ended horribly, with the twins withering and screaming in pain. Then, gangrene developed and they died after suffering for 3 long days and nights.

About three thousand pairs of twins lost their lives at Auschwitz at the hands of Josep Mengele.

The twins were often injected with various chemicals and even force-fed poisons to see their effect on them. Mengele injected them about three times a week and then studied the effects of the injected drugs or poisons on them.

After a period of time, Eva fell really ill after she was given five injections containing various poisons, drugs and serums. Her arms and legs swelled up and were almost double their normal size. Dr. Konig, Mengele and the other "doctors" in the facility took one look at her and deduced that she had at the most two weeks to live more.

Eva has said, "Doctor" Mengele looked at her fever chart and laughed loudly and said, "*Too bad, she is so young. She has only two weeks to live.*"

Eva knew that if she died, her sister Miriam would be useless for them and they would kill her too. So, she clung on to life and convinced herself that she needed to survive and live, so that her sister could live too. She was severely ill and often lost consciousness. She was so weak that she couldn't even get up and often resorted to crawling to the water faucet, but she did not give up hope. She clung on to life for her dear sister and survived through the ordeal.

The twins were in Auschwitz for nine months and were liberated by the Soviets when they took over the concentration camps. They also are the first pair of twins who have been featured in the movies made by the Soviets that showed the horrors of these concentration camps.

After being liberated, the sisters traveled to Israel, where they entered the Israeli army. Miriam studied and developed into a nurse, but sadly died in 1993 due to a rare form of cancer, probably brought upon her by the various chemicals and drugs injected into her body.

Eva studied drafting and went on to marry an American tourist named Michael Kor. Eva's life is riddled with the after effects of the torture she faced at the concentration camp and she suffers from tuberculosis and had a number of miscarriages. Her son also suffered from cancer.

Eva founded Terre Haute's Holocaust Museum and Education Center and also the founder of an organization commonly referred to as CANDLES. *It's an organization for the children who survived the experiments at Auschwitz*. She has also written books detailing her experiences at the Auschwitz camp.

Chapter 12: Jack Mandelbaum – Prisoner Number 16013

13-year-old Jack Mandelbaum lived in the port city of Gdynia. He was still living there as Germany began its expansive manoeuvres in August 1939. As the threat of Nazi invasion of Poland loomed on the horizon, Mandelbaum's father made the most difficult decision of his life – he sent away his wife and three children to the countryside to live with their relatives, in order to keep them safe. He promised them that he would follow them within the next six weeks after taking care of all of their pending matters.

There was no contact from their father, as they lived under the constant threat of Nazi invasion, until almost a year and half later. A postcard arrived, letting them know that their father had been caught and sent to a concentration camp in Stutthof. That was the last ever contact that he made – he died later in the concentration camp.

Jack Mandelbaum's only sister and the Mandelbaum's only daughter were killed while she was forced to march to a concentration camp with the masses. It is believed that she fell over and was trampled under the feet of the people marching to the concentration camp.

In June 1942 it finally happened what they had been dreading since August 1939. On 14th June 1942, just before dawn, the SS came and banged on the doors of the house, demanding that everyone present in the house step out within 5 minutes. They were herded in a queue in the marketplace and marched to the local brewery.

As they walked, an SS officer diverted the people from the line to the left or to the right. Jack hung on to his mother, as did his younger brother as they made their way towards the left. That was when something happened that changed Jack's life altogether.

The SS officer was going through the files of the arrested people and he realized that Jack had some experience in working as an electrician's helper. He immediately ordered that Jack be sent to the right. Jack struggled and moaned and clung on to his mother but to no avail. He was forcefully sent to the right and that was when he got the last glimpse of his mother and brother.

Unknown to him the, the SS officer had just saved his life by sending him to the right. The people who were marched towards the left were directly sent to an Auschwitz gas chamber and were gassed, while the people who were sent to the right were sent to the labor camps. Though it was hard labor and the state that they lived in was bad, at least they lived.

Jack was first sent to work at a granite quarry near Gross-Rosen. The barracks that they lived in were extremely overcrowded with prisoners and sometimes it was absolutely impossible to move a muscle while there. There were no beds, nor other furniture, and they all slept on the hard concrete.

For meals they were given a single piece of bread and some extremely dreadful tasting soup made using grass. Prisoners were inspected on a regular basis and all those that looked weak were sent away to be eliminated. To prevent getting killed, many of the prisoners adapted several measures like stuffing their mouths with crumpled paper so that their cheeks looked plump and they weren't exterminated.

While stuck in the concentration camp Jack always dreamed of being freed and going back to his "regular" life with his parents and siblings. News of Hitler's plans of exterminating all the Jews had not reached them and all the prisoners at the quarries thought that they would be freed one day. This ignorant hope was all that helped them survive.

He was transferred around to seven concentration camps in the 3 years that he was held prisoner. He had no name, no identity- just a prisoner number 16013.

The camp he was in when he was freed was one of the camps that was not "freed", but the German soldiers just disappeared overnight from there, leaving their prisoners behind. Unlike Auschwitz, which was freed by the Allied forces, his camp was left as it is as it was in the no man's land between the marching Russian forces and the absconding Nazi forces.

Finding themselves freed of their oppressors; Jack and a friend got into an abandoned horse carriage and rode away. While riding away they came across a women's concentration camp that still had people locked in it. Jack and his friend unlocked the doors, liberating them.

Jack had been 15 when he was taken to the concentration camp and he was 17 by the time he got out. He had lost almost 80 pounds working in various camps and surviving on those meagre meals.

After getting liberated he traveled through Poland looking for his family, but to no avail. He came across an uncle, but he was all he found. He then immigrated to and settled in Kansas, where he remained tight-lipped about his experiences in the concentration camps for a long 16 years, until he finally broke his silence and let it all go.

The book Surviving Hitler: A Boy in the Nazi Death Camps (2004) was written by Andrea Warren is based on Jack Mandelbaum's experiences in the concentration camps through the three years that he was imprisoned.

Chapter 13: Anita Laker-Wallfisch – Playing For Time

She was only a teenager, living with her family in Breslau, Germany, when Anita Lasker-Wallfisch was interned at Auschwitz. She credits her survival to the fact she could play the cello. By virtue of this skill, she was conscripted into Maria Mandl's all woman orchestra.

"We all knew what was going on there", she has said. "The odor of death was over us at all times. We knew the smoke billowing from the chimneys was what was left of other prisoners, as the incinerators burned day and night".

Anita had been unable to do anything to intervene as one by one, her family was deported to the camps. First her father and mother and then, her grandfather, as well as her aunt and uncle. Left behind in the family home with her sister, all Anita could was wonder when her number would come up.

"We were terrified every waking moment. Our family had been spirited away by this evil gripping Europe and we were helpless to do anything about it", she relates.

Anita and her sister decided that moving was preferable to staying where they were, alone and vulnerable and awaiting arrest. They felt they'd have a better chance if they left, so they attempted to leave Germany for France.

"We were caught, though. I'd tucked away a dose of cyanide for a moment just like this, terrified at the prospect of falling into the clutches of the Nazis. Many decided that suicide was better than the fate that awaited us in the concentration camps and so I took the dose. Fortunately, the person who'd given it to me had filled the capsules with icing sugar and not the poison I'd wanted".

Anita has described her eventual deportation and the horror of the intake process at the camp:

"After being detained for some time, we were placed on a transport to Auschwitz. There I learned the meaning of having my humanity taken from me.

We were ordered to strip naked. Then they shaved my head and my arm was tattooed with a number. This was not worse than being stripped of my hair. The anonymity of a sea of prisoners, all denuded of the hair on their heads, was strikingly dehumanizing. I felt I had ceased to exist."

During the registration process, Anita told the prisoner taking down her information that she played the cello. When she heard the response to this news, she was quite surprised.

"You'll survive, in that case," said the registration clerk.

The orchestra was stationed at the gate to the camp. Anita played a variety of music as part of this ensemble, as the other inmates left in the morning for work details. Music was also played at the end of the work day, when the prisoners returned. Sundays were reserved for special concerts.

Even though Anita enjoyed a special status at the camp due her participation in the orchestra, she was not immune to the daily roll calls and the conditions in which these were held.

"It didn't matter how sick you were. Unless you were dead, you were forced to participate in the incessant demands of the guards to present yourself to be counted and sorted by them, like livestock. We would have to stand there for many hours in whatever condition we were in. It was cold, wet and misery doesn't even begin to describe the nature of the experience".

Anita had given her shoes to another inmate. These were very distinctive and when her sister arrived at Auschwitz and saw them on the feet of the woman Anita had given them too, she immediately knew these were her sister's. She asked the prisoner wearing them where they'd come from. Anita explains that this is how they found each other again in the enormous facility:

"If the prisoner I'd given the shoes to hadn't told my sister that I played in the orchestra, we might not have ever known the other was there".

In 1944, Anita was transferred to Bergen-Belsen and was there until the camp was liberated at the end of the war. She was to travel to England in 1946 with her sister. There she found that people were unable to grasp the enormity of the Holocaust. She found their attitudes to be so dismissive that she kept her experiences almost entirely to herself. It seemed they were unable to absorb the enormity of genocide, or the presence of those who'd survived it.

Anita didn't return to Germany for more than a half century. In a recent interview she said:

"Anti-Semitism continues to exist, which is incredible to me in light of the horror it unleashed on the world in the 1940s. It's incredibly naïve to believe it has been eradicated."

For the sake of her ability to play a musical instrument. Anita survived. Having played for time, it was the meeting of the bow with the strings of the cello that saved her.

Chapter 14: Jakob Blankitny – The Man to Whom Life Gave Multiple Chances

Jakob Blankitny inhabited a small town known as Makow Mazowiecki, which was, located about 80 kilometers away from the city of Warsaw in Poland. When the German attack on Poland began, it saw the rise in several ghettos and labor camps and also brought with it the severe persecution of the Jews in the region.

In 1941, Germany broke its peace treaty with USSR and invaded the Eastern side of Poland that was under the power of the Soviets. Within a couple days, the invading Germans reached the town of Makow Mazowiecki and started making use of the town synagogue as their personal stable and demolished all symbols representing Jewish culture that they came across.

The Jews were ordered to always have David's star on them with the word "Jew" written in the middle of the star. This, they reasoned, would make it easy to recognize who the Jews were.

The Jews were arrested and sent to various labor camps, and from there they were transferred to concentration camps and also to ghettos to live in terrible circumstances. These ghettos had become a center for typhus and malnutrition and most of the elderly prisoners and children died in these camps.

After about two weeks, the prisoners were transferred into Mlawa's ghetto. The ghetto was empty because all its prior residents had been parceled off to Auschwitz. For 10 days, the prisoners lived here, working on various building tasks, until they were moved somewhere else.

All the women who had small children and the elderly prisoners were sent off to Treblinka, while the remaining prisoners were sent on their way to Auschwitz two days later. The circumstances in which they marched towards their doom were terrible.

Blankitny recollected that he'd never forget the favors his mother exchanged with the German soldiers for a half glass of water. He says he was only 16 and yet, *"my ears echo the painful cries of the thousands of people there."*

On arrival to Auschwitz, the men and women were immediately divided. All the women, including the sister and mother of Blankitny, were sent to a chamber to be gassed and further on to the crematoria.

The men were further divided into two groups and thankfully Blankitny's father and he were together in the group. Suddenly Blankitny and his father heard a cry from his uncle, beckoning them to the other group. Narrowly missing the German soldiers and their angry dogs, the duo made it to the other side and not a minute too soon. The group they had just left was sent to the gas chambers, while their new group was being led to Auschwitz-Birkenau.

Over 5,000 had entered Auschwitz that day, by the end of the day only 200 survived – Jakob Blankitny and his father were in the "lucky" 200 who survived. This was a common practice in Auschwitz as the number of prisoners was too high and the camps were getting too full. The camps were already full and with thousands more arriving every day, a major portion was gassed at random.

On entering Auschwitz, the prisoners were marked with their identifying numbers which would later become their only identity. It was during winter months when they entered the camp and the whole camp was muddy and flooded. All their winter wear was confiscated and all they were provided were light and thin clothes that resembled pajamas adorned with stripes. Each passing day, as their body weakened, the exact effect of being in camp could be gauged through the clothes that they had been provided.

The prisoners were sent to the barracks where there were triple bunk beds. Each bed was allotted to four people – each bed made for three accommodated 12 prisoners each.

Each morning the prisoners were woken up at 5 am and provided with some coffee and just one slice of bread. Then like animals the prisoners were counted to ensure that none of the prisoners had escaped or gone missing. The prisoners were beaten up on a regular basis, especially if any of them fell over or fell out of line.

The prisoners were made to work outside until 7 in the evening. When they returned to their bunks they were given soup, but only about about a quarter of a liter.

Jakob Blankitny and his father were luckily placed in the same barracks and their first job was to dig a water canal. Every evening they brought back 3 or 4 dead bodies of their co-prisoners, who were immediately sent off to the crematoria. Every day there were new selections and those who were sick were killed directly.

During one such selection the prisoners were asked their professions. Jakob said that he was in carpentry, while his father said he laid bricks. This information was what led to his father's demise. A few days after the selection, those who said they were carpenters were transferred elsewhere.

When he bid his father adieu, his father sent him away, telling him he would never see him again. The father's hope was that he could stay where he was and pass as a sick person, while the son had another chance by going elsewhere. He said:

"Though I am abandoning you, you have an obligation to go and save yourself."

With those last words Blankitny left his father and he would never see him again. They were transferred to Auschwitz I, where the commander did not believe Blankitny's lie of being in carpentry, then beat him up. He was sent off to do railroad work, where he was enslaved to unpack the wagons and carry enormous amounts of weight on his back.

While working there Blankitny contracted a horrible infection of the intestines and working in the bitter winter had resulted in his flesh falling off his fingers and his feet getting frostbitten.

He had carved a bathtub from wood outside the camp and once when late in returning, he was beaten with a log and then carried back to the barrack on the stretcher and thrown at the wall. When his friends returned in the evening, they helped him onto his bunk. The next morning he was taken to the hospital where his fellow prisoners helped bandage his feet up.

When the "Angel of Death", Josep Mengele, visited the hospital, he survived another selection by grouping with the mentally ill. The others were sent off to Birkenau, and immediately killed. Knowing that if there was another batch selected he wouldn't survive it, he convinced a doctor to let him go. The doctor knew that there was going to be another selection and let him go out of pity.

Malnourished and tired, he limped to his block, where his friends didn't even recognize him anymore. He worked for a few days in the camp and when there was an order for wood carvers to come ahead, he went on, having learned woodcarving in school.

The wood carvers were then transferred to D.A.V, the camp where the major locksmith and carpentry workshops were. Jakob hoped that the heat from the furnaces would help heal his feet. He made wooden spoons to be sent off to camps for Russians, as they were not allowed metal spoons for the fear of them being made into weaponry. They were supposed to meet a certain number within 2 weeks – one that Jakob was unable to meet.

He was banished from the factory and made to carry planks of heavy wood to workshops and return with heavy boxes of sawdust. If they were too slow when working, they were brutally beaten up; and the brutal beating was an enough motivation to keep him going fast and hard.

Any remaining Polish laborers were reassigned to various other camps, leaving lots of machinery unmanned. Jakob was spotted by the factory's capo and was shown how the machinery worked. He also told Jakob that if he worked well he could stay. Jakob quickly caught on and kept working there until 1945.

With the arrival of the Russians looming in the distance, the Germans rounded up all the prisoners and made them walk to a train station almost 90 kilometers away from where they were. Thousand people left the camp, but only half of them arrived at the train station. The other half died in the march through the snow.

Upon reaching the station, they were loaded into open wagons that were on their way to Mauthausen. Even here almost half of the prisoners died as they could not bear the winter conditions in the open wagons and froze to death. The survivors were transported to Melk and were made to work in the mines there until the spring of 1945.

This was when the Americans started moving in towards defeating the Germans. The prisoners were moved to a camp known as Ebensee in Upper Austria. While on their way there, many of the prisoners managed to escape. When the remaining prisoners arrived at the camp, they were only 20 in number. They were in a line, waiting to be shot when a commander approached the soldiers with the guns saying *"They are not even worth the bullet. No matter - they will die in the camp."*

The prisoners were provided with only a meal per day – which consisted mostly of soup. Peels from the potatoes were also provided, along with table scraps the SS left behind. About 500 to 600 prisoners died each day.

On 4th May the American army closed in and all the prisoners were ordered to the mine for "protection", but rumors flew around that this was the plan to incinerate the 10,000 odd prisoners, as the mines were full of explosives.

The prisoners rebelled against the German SS and they no longer had the power to control them. The SS left, locking the prisoners in the camp behind them. Civilian guards came over for the prisoners and the morning afterward, the tanks came in with American soldiers, liberating them on 5th May 1945. Blankitny and his co-prisoners were the last people to be liberated from the clutches of the Holocaust.

4,000 odd Jews lived in Makow Mazowiecki before the German invasion began. Jakob Blankitny was one of the 42 people who survived the ordeal. Jakob was also the sole survivor from his immediate and extended family.

Chapter 15: Rena Kornreich – Sister Survivors

Rena Kornreich was the 716th Jewish woman to be interned at the Auschwitz concentration camp. At the age of 21, she was part of a group of almost 1,000 young women to be deported to the camp. This was the first group of Jewish women to arrive there.

Rena had already seen what the Nazis were capable of, in Poland. She knew her deportation was a turning point and one which didn't bode well for her and the others who'd been deported. She did not, however, have any idea about the depths of the depravity she was about to witness as a prisoner at Auschwitz.

Almost the moment she arrived, she was to get a taste of it. She asked a guard how the prisoners would find their baggage, and in response, he screamed:

"You're not here to ask questions! Get back with the others!"

It was at that moment she understood that the guard saw her as something less than human. The incident left her in shock at the possibility of being completely divested of every right humans normally enjoy. In an instant, she was made privy to the pervasive power of ideological indoctrination and its effect on people.

Shortly after Rena arrived at the camp, her sister, Danka, arrived. The two of them were interned for the next three years. During their internment, they were to be part of the complex of slave labor the Nazis had built.

The two of them were eventually sent to neighboring Birkenau. There, they were selected by the infamous Dr. Mengele to work in the laundry dedicated solely to managing the laundry SS personnel. With this, they were removed from the more grisly aspects of camp life and were certainly more secure than those still in the general population.

While Rena was working the laundry, she was to have an experience rarely documented in accounts of the Holocaust. She was to meet the infamous Irma Grese. The following is one of the very few accounts in existence from a woman survivor, concerning a Third Reich women executed for her crimes against humanity.

"Irma Grese was notorious throughout the camp. Her reputation for pathological violence struck fear into everyone when she appeared. One day as I was hanging laundry outside to dry, she approached me.

"We have plans for you Jews. When the Third Reich achieves world domination..."

He went on to ask if we knew what they were going to do with us. Grese looked at me quite pointedly, expecting a response.

"I have no idea", I said. The woman's presence sent a chill down my spine.

"We're sending you to an island. There, you will be slaves, serving the Fatherland. You'll be neutered, of course, to prevent any possibility of you reproducing".

"My mind was numb with the horror of her words, yet these weren't even delivered maliciously. She was so matter of fact, as though she were reciting a grocery list. I couldn't conceive of it – lifelong slavery. I avoided her eyes, as I made to return to the laundry, but I could feel them on my back as I walked away, watching me; waiting for some kind of indication that her words had incited an almost unbearable horror in me. I wanted to fall to pieces. I wanted to shriek senselessly. I wanted all this to end and for my life to be as it had been, when I'd been free.

And then it dawned on me that the future was not yet written. That only this day mattered. The thought that Grese had no more idea what was going to happen next that I did displaced the disgust I felt. This thought was liberating. It also made of Grese a fool."

In the middle of the bitter winter of 1945, the two sisters left Auschwitz forever. Still prisoners, they were driven in a raging blizzard with other inmates and marched to Wodzislaw Slaski.

For almost a week, they marched through the freezing conditions, finally arriving after having marched over 50 kilometers. They were then taken to central Germany on train cars intended to haul coal.

Rena and her sister were to dig ditches for the remainder of the war. These were intended to hold back the Allies, but were also used as mass graves for other prisoners. Many died on this death march, either of starvation or abuse at the hands of their oppressors. Some were shot.

Then, the Allies came and the two sisters were finally set free.

Rena and Danka had survived the horror of Auschwitz. Sisterhood is said to be powerful. In the case of these two survivors, it's obviously miraculous.

Chapter 16: Solomon Radasky – The Furrier With A Happy Ending

Solomon Radasky lived in Praga and owned his own shop where he would make and sell fur coats. Out of his family of 78 people, which included his parents Jacob and Toby, brothers Baruch and Moishe and his sisters Leah, Sarah and Rivka, Solomon was the only one who survived the Holocaust.

After the German invasion he and his family were arrested and sent to live in one of the ghettos that the invading Germans had set up. They were forced to live and work there in unbearable conditions, where slowly he saw his family die, one by one.

His mother and elder sister were shot dead in the last week of January in the year 1941, when Solomon was forced by the SD and the Jewish police to work on the railroad, clearing the snow off it and ensuring that the trains didn't stop running. When he returned to the ghetto he was informed that the Germans had ordered the Judenrat (a Jewish council set up by the Germans) to collect gold and furs from the people in the ghetto. When Radasky's mother claimed she had none to give, they shot her and his older sister too.

His father was killed in April 1942. Children often smuggled food like potatoes, bread, and cabbages into the ghetto across the wall that separated the ghetto from the other parts of the city. His father was buying bread from such children when a Jewish man pointed him out to a German. The German immediately shot his father in the back.

On 22nd July 1942, the Germans started deporting people from the ghetto to various concentration camps. It was then that Radasky's two other sisters and two brothers were deported to Treblinka. He never saw any of his family again.

He began working at Tobben's shop as a furrier, providing fur for the German army. This proved to be a good decision, because when he was selected to be sent to a concentration camp, his master came to his rescue and vouched for him to be a good worker.

Sometime later a friend informed him that he had seen one of his sisters working at Shultz's shop. He arranged for a German soldier to take him there and bring him back safely for about 500 zlotys. Despite reaching there and looking for his sister everywhere, he could not find her. Saddened, he tried to return to the ghetto, but he couldn't as the German soldiers had it surrounded.

The date was 19 April 1943. The Warsaw Ghetto Uprising was beginning.

On the 1st of May 1943, Radasky was shot in the ankle. Thankfully it was a flesh wound and it didn't have any lasting effect on his leg. He was sent to the Treblinka concentration camp, but as the camp could only accommodate 10,000 people and their train had 20,000, their train was cut into half. The first half was sent to Treblinka, while the other half was sent to Majdanek.

Radasky was a part of the group that was sent to Majdanek.

At Majdanek they were provided with clothes and he was sent to Barracks 21. There a fellow inmate had managed to smuggle a pocketknife into the concentration camp. He decided to help Radasky by operating upon him, but warned him saying that he had no medicine or bandages and whenever he were to urinate, he should use his own urine to disinfect his wound.

The Majdanek prisoners were made to walk 3 kilometers every day, in order to reach the place of their work. Majdanek was one of the death camps where every little mistake resulted in death. To hide his wound from the sentries at the gates of the camp Radasky would ensure that he did not limp in front of them or else he would be hanged.

The prisoners were provided with heavy wooden shoes. They were told to remove the shoes as soon as they left the camp and hang them around their necks on a string for the whole 3-kilometer walk. The path was strewn with rocks and stones that cut into the feet of the prisoners. Many of them who couldn't take it anymore would fall over. Those who didn't get up quickly were shot dead. Then the rest of the prisoners had to carry the body to work and back to the camp – 1,000 left the camp and 1,000 had to come back!

While working, chain smokers often lit a piece of paper they could find in order to emulate the feel of smoking. Once a German officer caught the whiff of the smoke and demanded to know who was smoking. When no one gave him an answer he selected 10 people to kill. Radasky one of them.

He was made to stand on the bench with two other with ropes around their necks. The German officer beat them using a whip. He kept beating them until they were bleeding.

Radasky would have died, if not for another German soldier who had come to Majdanek to collect the three selected groups of 750 each that were to be transferred to another camp. Radasky was one of.

The next morning he was put on a train to transfer him to the next camp. In the 9 weeks that Radasky had lived in Majdanek he had not changed his clothes nor bathed. He had lice and he was swollen due to the lack of food.

After two nights and a day when he got off the train, he realized that he had been taken to Auschwitz. A few of the prisoners were selected and machine gunned down in front of them. They were no longer taking the trouble of sending the selected ones to the gas chamber.

Radasky was then tattooed with the number 128232. After getting his tattoo, he was given one potato to eat. He was then quarantined at Buna and then sent to work at the railroad tracks. The capo there was a sadistic man and often paired short workers with tall ones so that the tall partner had to bend his knees while carrying 20 feet long iron.

One time Radasky fell over and due to the extreme malnutrition and weakness he couldn't stand up. The capo beat him up brutally. During the next selection, he was made to stand naked in the cold all night long. The next day he and the other selected ones were loaded into a truck with a red cross on it. He thought he was being taken to the gas chamber, but in reality he was taken to Auschwitz I.

There he met a man named Elrich who had been with him at Majdanek. Elrich informed him that he was in the hospital barracks and "Doctor" Mengele often did rounds here, selecting people. When he had first gotten there five weeks ago, two doctors who had recognized him because they knew his grandfather had hid him and other Jews. The SS had arrived and killed all the Jews and the two doctors too.

After two days of rest, Elrich informed him that he had to escape or else he would be killed. On hearing this, Radasky went into panic and blindly accepted the first job offered to him, in an attempt to get out of the hospital.

He made new friends with his new bunkmates and bonded with them over someone from his hometown that they all knew. Sadly, this new job that he had blindly accepted was working in a coal mine and his new friends informed him that no one survived the job more than two weeks.

One of his new friends had some influence with the Capo as they smuggled out valuables such as cigarettes and salami and provided them to the capo. The capo agreed to turn a blind eye to the fact that Radasky did not show up for his assigned work, provided he didn't get caught sneaking out with the rest.

He would walk in the middle with his friends who would cover him and save him from prying eyes. All the while he was there he stayed with his new friends and they provided him with bread and soup.

One day, one of his friends asked him if he could sew a cap for the Capo. Using a strip of cloth Radasky made a cap for him, and the Capo loved it. From then on Radasky became the Capo's man and he was never beaten in his time at Auschwitz again.

Radasky's job was to dig sand in the sand mines and load it all up in wagons. Then, they had to push the wagon almost 16 kilometers. Twice a day they would push the sand filled wagons to Birkenau to pour sand over the ashes of the dead. The ovens were on the other side of the crematoria; hence the ash came out on this side. The gas chamber was on the other side of the ovens.

Radasky did this job for almost a year. While he was working, he saw transports filled with people arrive. He watched as people were divided into two – left and right. He saw all those people before they were forced into the gas chamber. In August and September 1944 he actually saw them grab live children and throw them into the crematorium.

One day while they were working a soldier with a rifle appeared. Scared, they started to rush around. It was then that the Hungarian soldier informed them that they were to go to his barracks at 4 o'clock and check his trash where he would keep 11 pieces of bread for them. In return he wanted money from Canada.

Canada was a place in Auschwitz – Birkenau where the belongings of those who were deported were kept. Canada had mounds of blankets, pots, pans, prams, trunks, gold, food, etc., and these items were sorted and sent over to Germany to boost the morale of the German citizens.

It was a good arrangement, but one day the officer suddenly disappeared.

The Russians were pushing the Germans hard at Stalingard and people were being deported mercilessly from the Lodz ghetto. Then the Hungarians were being deported and gassed at a quick rate.

A group of young people wanted to destroy the crematoria. There were four of them at Birkenau. The girls who worked at the ammunition factory managed to smuggle in some explosives and blow up one crematorium. They hung 2 of the girls in public view as a warning for the rest.

The liquidation of Auschwitz started on 18th January 1945. Radasky was forced to leave a mere 7 days before the Russians liberated it. He started walking with a Rabbi, saving his life and pulling him on a sled with a companion. Many people who fell during this walk were shot.

Having a Rabbi with him ensured that he could retain some of his Jewish culture and Kaddish for his parents.

At dawn they reached a small town where the farmers let them stay in the stable. In the evening they were shooed out. They walked to the railroad station and took a train for two days to Gross-Rosen. He never saw the Rabbi ever again.

Gross-Rosen was overfull with almost 2,000 people jammed into a single shed. In the day the stood all day, while at night the slept on each others' feet. They were just given a single slice of bread and coffee at night.

He was then marched to the railroad station and took a 3-day train ride to Dachau. They were forced to eat snow for water. People went crazy on the train and a son choked his own father. At Dacahu there was a selection and a lot of people disappeared.

He left Dachau and was made to board a death train. After reaching a field they were all asked to get off the train. When they got off, German soldiers fired at them with machine guns. A few hundred died, while the rest ran back to the safety of the train.

As the Americans were bombing the area, prisoners were called upon to clear the area. When no one volunteered, Radasky and two others were randomly chosen. Radasky was sure he would die like his family and decided he wouldn't die hungry. He stole a piece of bread at the train station he was supposed to be cleaning and kept eating it despite the fact that the officer in charge was beating him up brutally.

After he ate his bread he went back to work and once his work was done he was sent back to the train. The next morning he heard chaos and rushed to the window. The expected to see the Russians but they saw the Americans. They hollered and celebrated.

The Americans freed them on 1st May 1945, making them some of the last Holocaust prisoners freed.

The Americans provided the prisoners with rice, but the MP did not allow them to eat it, as it would have killed them. He explained that their stomachs had shrunk in size and eating something laden with fat would kill them. He asked them to eat toast for a few days before furthering onto heavier foods. The American MPs also provided the prisoners with clothes, shoes and other basic amenities.

He later met his future wife through a former business associate. He loaned money and arranged for stamps to get himself a suit, exchanged two Hershey bars, two packets of cigarettes, and a coffee can with a German woman for a dress for his wife and got married to her.

They soon moved to New Orleans, and he got a job in fur shop without knowing a word of English. He was underpaid in the beginning, but he worked hard and went on to work for the Haspel Brothers. He educated and raised two children with his wife.

There were about 375,000 Jews who lived in Warsaw before the war broke out. By the time the war and the Holocaust ended there were next to none left. Today, there are fewer than 5,000 Jews living in Warsaw today.

Chapter 17: Mara Ginic & Her Companions – Who Crossed Mountains to Escape Persecution

Mara Ginic was originally from Yugoslavia, and was born in a town named Zagreb in 1925. When she was about four years old, she moved in with her grandparents to Ojisek in Slavonia. After her parents got divorced when she was five, she continued to live with her father and grandparents in Ojisek. When she was eight they moved to Belgrade, where she lived with her father and stepmother.

After Hitler's occupation of Belgrade in April 1941, Mara and her father succeeded in escaping to Hvar, a Croatian island, with the help of her mother who was an ethnic German and Catholic. Hvar proved to be extremely unsafe for them as it was under the Croat Ustashi. From there, they escaped to the Italian occupied island of Split, but they were arrested and deported to a town named Piedmont in the northern part of Italy as the civilian prisoners of war.

It was in September 1943 when the Germans occupied Northern Italy that Mara, her father and a few friends decided to flee to the mountains with the intention of crossing over to Switzerland. After an extremely dangerous attempt to cross the mountains on their own, they came across a guide in Breuil Cervinia. He descended from a long line of mountain climbers and Jean Antoine Carrel, the first Italian to climb the Matterhorn, was his grandfather.

Breuil is at the base of the Matterhorn, while their destination Zermatt, Switzerland was on the other side of the Matterhorn. After grabbing their backpacks and putting on their low shoes, they left at dawn with Carrel their guide. Another mountain guide joined their little group, adding two more men and three women to their group.

As they advanced, their trek became steeper. They walked in a single file with Carrel leading them and his colleague bringing up the rear. While walking

Carrel handed them a pill that fighter pilots usually consumed before going on tough assignments. It increased endurance.

Mara claims that after she consumed the pill her backpack felt as light as a feather and she felt like she was walking on clouds. She felt as though her feet were barely touching the ground.

As night descended upon them, the weather got nippier, forcing them to add warmer clothing. Mara mentions putting on mittens and even handing her father one of her own as he wasn't as equipped for the weather as she was. The uphill trek till dawn was quite easy, with the cold weather being the major challenge for them.

As they ascended, their path became narrower and had more stones on it. They were forced to carefully place their feet sideways, facing the steep rock and holding on to any little crevice they could.

Carrel fastened a rope over the steep step-like cliffs where they slid down the rope for several yards. After crossing this difficult phrase of their journey they arrived at the glacier. Carrel pointed straight ahead and told the group that was the direction they were to go. As they were at the border, he could no longer accompany them further.

He was paid the gold promised by her father's friend Hinko Salz and he and his companion left them alone with the path over the glacier ahead of them. They stood there for a few minutes, unsure of what to do, where to go and how to proceed, but soon they got over their fear and carried on.

The glacier was extremely cold and icy winds hit them with great force. The glacier was extremely smooth and would have been easy to cross if they hadn't worn mountain shoes. They also came across crevices. Most of them were small enough for them to just step over, but most of the times were large enough to warrant a jump across its two sides.

They had been walking for about 12 hours and the effects of the pill were wearing off. Every step was painful, every jump was another challenge and the backpacks seemed to pull them to the ground.

Their throats were dry and parched and incessant wind made it difficult for them to see ahead. Often their knees buckled under them and the glacier just seemed to go on and on. Mara found herself falling over frequently, and often she didn't have the strength to pick herself off the icy floor. Her father was exhausted too, but he pushed her to go on.

Her limbs were stiff from the cold and her fingers and toes felt like they would fall of any moment. Enough was enough – she was going nowhere! Her father tried to pick her off the floor and encourage her to go on, but her screaming caught him off guard. She had a nervous breakdown in the middle of the glacier, and her father, with a sign from Dr. Salc, slapped her hard across her face. The slap brought her back to her senses and they moved forward.

They soon made it over the glacier and arrived at a lake. Across the lake they could see a small hut – the border patrol. The guards from the guardhouse had been observing them for a while with their powerful binoculars and came forward to meet them.

They were taken to the guardhouse and provided with some water. It was then that the guards dropped the bomb – they couldn't stay there and had to turn back! They also learned that not only were the refugees turned away; sometimes they were also handed over to the Germans immediately.

Mara's father and Dr. Salc attempted to persuade the border guards to let us in. Mara's father even called his sister who lived in Switzerland, but even she was helpless as she was a refugee herself. Harrowed and defeated, they started begging. Even when tears didn't do the trick, the two other women fell to the feet of the guards, tearing their hair and creating such a scene that the superior officer called his own superiors. Deciding that the situation was too much for him to deal with alone and the group was to be sent to Zermatt.

They believed that once they entered the country they wouldn't be expelled. They didn't know that many of the refugees were handed over to the Germans by the Swiss Police, even if they had entered the country). Mara mentions in her account that she was so happy to be in the country free from oppression that she actually thought she was imagining the honey like smell in the air, only to realize that the guard walking with them was smoking a pipe.

They were put up in a hotel where they were able to get clean and comfortable with a warm bed after almost 24 hours of walking, climbing, and jumping.

The group became instant celebrities in Zermatt and were treated like heroes. People stopped them in the street and offered them fruits, chocolates, and cigarettes. Even on the train to the refugee camp, people kept handing them apples and cigarettes.

They remained in Switzerland until the war ended. Mara married Ivo Kraus there and made the decision to not return to Yugoslavia. Mara and her husband moved to Italy. She moved often and lived in places like Argentina, France, Venezuela, Brazil, Austria, and the United States.

She may not have faced the horrors of a concentration camp or set a foot in Auschwitz, but she and her companions were and are still considered to be the survivors of the Holocaust. The Holocaust is just not limited to the horrors of concentration camps. It begins with the horror of being persecuted for following a particular religion. It is being persecuted in your own home and having to live as a refugee in another country because of the twisted beliefs of others.

Chapter 18: Dora Sorell – An Odyssey

It was in 1940 that Hungary made its historic deal with the Devil.

In exchange for Hitler's return of northern Transylvania to Hungary, the nation's government agreed to collaborate with the Nazis and enter into an alliance with Germany.

Dora's village was located in the area given to the Hungarians and her world rapidly changed due to this unexpected and unwelcome development. What had been a peaceful existence was turned upside down by the mounting aggression of Hitler's Third Reich. Dora explains the new reality that grew up overnight for her, her family and neighbors:

"Once the former Romanian territory had been handed to the Hungarians, they began to impose new rules and regulations on us. There were new directives every day. They never favored us, of course. In fact, they made life very difficult and were deliberately intended to do so. It was almost impossible to run local businesses, which had to be at least partially Hungarian-owned. People were thrown out of work and the situation became increasingly desperate, as people's businesses were confiscated. Finally, Jewish children were no longer permitted to attend public schools."

As time went by, Hungarian actions against the Jews increased. Young Jewish men were being arrested and an organized resistance movement sprang up. Certain types of literature were banned (anything that might challenge Hungarian fascism, for example). Dora remembers the Hungarian soldiers coming for the young men of her town:

"They took my brothers and also, my boyfriend. My boyfriend was first taken to a camp for political dissidents. He was then tried and given five years as punishment for being a communist and imprisoned."

At this time, many of the young men taken by Hungarian fascist forces were drafted into the military. Dora's brother was one of them. All Jews drafted into the Hungarian Army were used as mine sweepers and ditch diggers on the war's front lines. Many of these young men were injured and died, they were consigned to the most dangerous work available. Dora's brother was very fortunate, indeed, to be spared this perilous duty, as she relates:

"The Hungarians discovered that Moishi was very intelligent and talented. For this reason, they saw a value in him and kept him in the administrative offices. There he made souvenirs for the soldiers. He also was fed more adequately than other prisoners. Right before we were deported, he returned to our village, alive and well."

In that same year, Dora Sorell graduated from high school. But it was not until the late winter of 1944 that Germany, having had enough of Hungary's demands concerning the Jews (that they remain in Hungary and be put to work there) invaded. Almost as soon as they arrived, the Germans began to document all Jews in the country. Working from these lists, the Germans moved from Jewish home to Jewish home, confiscating the valuables of those who lived in them and commandeering the same homes for use as offices. All Jews were forced to wear a yellow star on their coats or jackets at this time.

Dora recalls her father's question to a German officer. *"What's going to happen to us,"* he asked. The German responded, in dulcet tones:
"Germans are decent people. Don't worry."

Confused and terrified by the rapid descent of their lives into the chaos of ethnic cleansing, Dora and her family found themselves forced into a ghetto on the outskirts of her town. Romanian and Hungarian gentiles took over what had once been Jewish homes. All the Jews in Dora's village were instructed to pack only one bag and to bring a supply of food to last two weeks.

The ghetto had a gate that prevented anyone from leaving. There, the Jews were crowded together, small rooms being shared by as many as ten families. There was neither heat nor hot water in these living quarters. The ghetto had no shops or medical services. Nonetheless, the local hospital was emptied out and the sick shoved into the tiny ghetto. Without access to professional medical care, many of these people died.

But the ghetto was to be short-lived. Only two weeks after its establishment, the Hungarian Army moved to deport those living in it to Auschwitz. Dora describes the scene on the morning of the deportation:

"We'd been instructed to be outside on the morning we were to leave. There were thousands of us in the streets. People were fighting. Babies and children were weeping. After we'd all been out there for some time, milling about and exchanging ideas about where we thought we were going, the Hungarians signaled we were to be moved out of the ghetto.

Without warning, soldiers began to force us out, beating us and screaming at the top of their lungs, as they came at us like wild animals. Older people stumbled and fell and people helpless to defend themselves dropped the one bag they'd been allowed to bring, where it was trampled by the feet of thousands running from these monsters. My family managed to stay together through this nightmare.

The entire way, we saw the discarded belongings of those who'd put their hands up in self-defense. Pieces of their shattered lives littered the road. When we'd finally run the gruesome Nazi gauntlet and arrived at the place were to be loaded for transport, we were told to wait. And wait we did, as the train failed to arrive.

When it finally arrived, we saw that the train was made up of cars designed to transport cattle. The soldiers began dividing us into groups to be loaded into the cars, which were just empty boxes. Families were split up as we were pushed into the cars and locked in. No light. No food. No water. A bucket serving as a toilet for about 80 of us.

I could hear my mother weeping. My father did his best to comfort her, as my family huddled together on the floor. We were sitting almost on top of each other in the overcrowded cattle car. There was no way to sleep in this horrible place. The stench from the bucket was overwhelming. We were hungry. The thirst was incredible. For three days, we stayed there, with the only relief being the emptying of the bucket at major stops along the way."

The train rolled on toward Auschwitz until finally, it stopped. Anxious to see where they were, the people inside strained to see what they could of the place they'd been taken. As night fell, the occupants of the cattle cars had little knowledge of where they were. Dora remembers her arrival:

"The darkness closed in and none of us was any the wiser as to where we had wound up. We were shut inside the cattle car in the night. After some time, the train began to move. I now know this was when we moved into the camp itself.

We were moving for only a few moments, when we stopped again. There was a sudden clamor of activity outside. Then the door flew open onto the gates of hell.

Guards were yelling at us to get off the train. The night was filled with barked orders in German, the growling of the guard dogs and gunshots. I heard the cries of children in the midst of it.

We were told to leave our belongings in the cattle car. This is the first time I saw the sondercommandos (Jewish inmates used by the Germans to control the camp's prisoners…and sow division among them). Everything we left behind on the train began to be piled up on the tracks in front of the train's engine.

Everyone was finally out of the cars and I saw that I was part of a vast multitude gathered there. Everyone was panicked; grappling for space and disoriented. All around us, families were being separated, as the night was filled with the pungent scent of smoke. I couldn't comprehend the horror of what was happening to us.

At this point, the intake process commenced in earnest, with the Germans sorting the new arrivals. The first division was made between men and women.

I watched as my brothers and my father were consumed by the sea of people around us. That was the last time I was to ever see them," Dora remembers.

Following the sorting process, all the new prisoners were moved off into separate areas. This was the first time Dora saw Dr. Mengele. Standing on a dais, with other SS officers, he seemed to be directing the crowd:

"I could see him up ahead in the electric light over the dais. He was telling the younger women and girls to proceed one way and the older women, in another. This is when my mother completely broke down. Having just watched her husband and sons torn away from her, she was now to see the same done to me.

I decided I was going to stay with my mother and tried to mimic the appearance of a middle-aged women, but the guards would have none of it. They yelled at me to go in the direction of the other young women and girls, but I didn't respond. At this, one of them struck me with a wooden baton with all his force, causing me to lose my grasp of my mother's arm. They then began to push me in the opposite direction. The last time I saw her, she was sobbing, full of grief and pain. This is how Auschwitz forced me to remember my mother for the rest of my life."

But the brutal selection process of the Nazis was not over. Dora's group, now consisting of only young women and girls was driven through the night, chased by the Nazi guards, beating and yelling the whole time. It was on their arrival that the next phase of the selection process commenced, as Dora recalls:

"The drove us toward a large outbuilding. As we entered it, they ordered us to stand around the edges of the walls, flush with them. We were then ordered to remove our clothes and put them in the middle of the large room we were in. We were permitted to keep our shoes on.

An older prisoner then went to each of us and said we had to remove any jewelry we were wearing. They took it all.

But the woman coming around for our jewelry noticed that the shoes I had on were flimsy and unsuitable for conditions in the camp. In an act of such kindness I will forget it, she offered me her own."

All prisoners had been completely denuded of their clothing and precious things. The next step of the intake process was to shave the heads of the new prisoners. Dora describes the dehumanizing effect this had on the women:

"Many of us had very long hair and to have it shaved off rendered us completely unrecognizable as the people we'd been walking in the gates. There was now a uniformity to us. Our individuality had been stripped from us as part of the Nazi program of removing all vestiges of humanity from concentration camp inmates."

Next, the new arrivals were herded into a shower facility, where they were given no soap and only a moment under the water. They were then issued their uniforms. Next, prisoners were lined up and a count was conducted. Of the thousands of women who'd arrived on the train, Dora recounts that only 421 remained.

For the seven months Dora was interned at Auschwitz, the days were a blur of hard work and little food to fuel prisoner efforts toward it. Starvation and malnutrition was a fact of life at the camp.

Slave labor is a life of utter misery in which the slave is considered an expendable piece of equipment. Dora remembers an incident at Auschwitz during which she was badly beaten by a guard for refusing to beat a fellow inmate in her work party:

"The summer I was in Auschwitz I worked in a team near the SS hospital. One day I remember the supervisor leaving me in charge of the other young women in the work party. Having been left in charge, I didn't want to be responsible for anyone getting in trouble with the guards, so I kept at them. When I saw a guard was near, I would yell at everyone to get to work when they needed to and to lay off when the coast was clear.

I didn't know I was being watched. In fact, one of the guards had been observing me and came out to my group from the hospital (where he'd been watching), absolutely furious. He complained bitterly about one of the women in particular and demanded that I beat her. I would not and so he took my hand and pulled it toward her face, but I refused. He then began to slap me across both sides of my face so hard, I almost fell over. When he was done, he demanded I do the same to this woman. Again, I didn't follow the order. One more time, he beat me. In his frustration at my disobedience, he left in a huff, but I was still standing. It was a miracle I wasn't shot dead on the spot for my insubordination".

As winter set in, work details were brought to a halt. This did little to alleviate the misery of life in Auschwitz. Dora remembers it as though it were yesterday:

"There was no end to our misery. The weather was freezing and with little to eat, our malnourished bodies weren't at all adaptable to it. With ill-fitting, improper footwear, our feet were covered in blisters. By this time, it was rumored that the Allies were on their way. We knew that we might be set free by the Allies, but it was also understood that the Germans would massacre us all, rather than let us speak of what they'd done."

The inmates knew things were about to take a turn for the worse. Work crews were being sought at other camps and Dora, being young and healthy, was anxious to be chosen for one of these. One day, during the selection, she had a flash of inspiration. Calling out in German that she knew how to draught plans, she was immediately chosen.

Because of her skill at draughting, Dora was able to leave Auschwitz for the Weisswasser work camp. This was just as the Third Reich was about to fall and the Nazis, in their desperation, were to conduct the infamous death marches and exterminations that marked the war's end.

At Weisswasser, Dora's experience of camp life improved dramatically. Living and working conditions, while grievously less than ideal, were not the nightmarish conditions of Auschwitz. Then on May 6, 1945, the Allies finally came and the work camp was liberated.

Dora has spent most of her life educating young people about the horrors of the Holocaust by telling her story. She has been tireless in her efforts to ensure that the acts of the Nazis are never forgotten and that humanity find ways not to repeat them. Her odyssey through the machinery of mass murder built by the Third Reich stands as timeless testimony against genocide.

Chapter 19: Elie Wiesel – The Nobel Laureate

Today, he is known as a winner of the Nobel Peace Prize, a novelist, a journalist and an activist. But in Auschwitz, Elie Wiesel was known as A7713. Like Dora Sorell, Elie lived in Romania, until the territory in which his town was located was handed to Hungary by Hitler, in 1942. Part of the agreement by which Hungary received northern Transylvania was that it would co-operate with the Nazis in their plan for the eventual extermination of the Jews.

When Elie was only 15, his town was occupied by the Germans. Abruptly, his studies came to a halt, including his new found interest in the mystical Kabbalah. It was 1944 and suddenly, the teenager found himself walking the streets of his town wearing a large yellow star, sewn by law to his jacket. Homes were raided, Jewish shops were closed and a ghetto created.

In the late spring of that year, the Hungarian deportation of the Jews began. Elie's family was one of the last to leave. On the cattle car they were loaded onto, there were at least 80 people. Later in his life, he was to write in one of his books that this was the moment at which being a teenager, full of life and curiosity, ended.

For four long days, the train the Wiesel family was on moved across Europe to its destination. He describes a woman from his village taking leave of her senses due to the horror of deportation, packed into a dark cattle car with almost 100 other people. Her hallucinations were shared with fellow deportees, with nothing to do but sit in the darkness listening to her ravings about seeing a fire outside the train. She was hallucinating, but the vision was oddly prophetic.

Finally arriving at Auschwitz II (Birkenau), Elie did as the prisoners conducting intake told him to and lied about his age, saying he was older. With his father, he was assigned to a work party. But the female members of his family were immediately sent to their deaths.

It was the sickly sweet smell that first assaulted him, as he left the cattle car, to stand on the platform at Birkenau. He knew it was the smell of human bodies roasting. He knew not only by the smell, but by the sight of the chimneys rising menacingly over the crematoria and the flames that issued from them.

"I believed the world was ending, at least for those of us who were Jewish. I felt the Apocalypse had arrived. The woman in the cattle car's hallucinations were all too prescient," he recalls.

Those prisoners marked for death were sent to the showers. Over time, Elie discovered that these were gas chambers, designed for the large scale extermination of human beings. Deadly Zyklon B would be thrown down a chute from outside the chamber. As the contents of the canisters met the air, they became cyanide, a lethal poison.

Death arrived slowly, with prisoners taking as long as a quarter of an hour to succumb to the gas. SS officers were known to watch the spectacle of death through peepholes cut in the walls for that purpose.

Elie recalls that as life in the camp unfolded, he became aware of its inhuman processes. He knew, eventually, that the step in the extermination process that followed the gas chambers was that of the bodies being removed for incineration. This step was left to Jewish prisoners. Those who were forced to do this were granted another day's life, but the horror of what they were doing drove many mad.

Wiesel's descriptions of Auschwitz depict a killing machine of massive scale, operated with the systematic precision of a timepiece. An obsession with order and efficiency became a mania within the camp's walls, facilitating death on a massive scale with increasing success. They were in the business of mass, politically-sanctioned murder and the Third Reich was good at it. In essence, the Nazis made an industry of killing. The industrialization of death is their only real legacy.

At night, bunks were stuffed with inmates, with a minimum of two sharing each, lying on straw. In the night, creeping things of all manner were everywhere, climbing on them. Disease was thus rampant. Every possible illness, due to the lack of camp hygiene, raged, at times taking out huge swathes of the camp population.

Even when the cold was at its most insupportable, prisoners were issued only the iconic striped cotton pajamas and nothing else. Food was scarce and insufficient to support human life. With the rigorous demand for forced labor, many people to died of starvation.

The life span of Auschwitz prisoners was only about four months. Due to the conditions described above, the goal of extermination and the violence that was ever present, attrition was at least one way in which the Nazis pursued the Final Solution.

Returning to Auschwitz with Oprah Winfrey to recount his experiences for a documentary on the camps, Professor Wiesel said:

"This place is filled with ghosts. They're even in the cracks in the walls and between the paving stones. Everywhere we go, I know I'll feel them, looking out at us from the grave. Even though they're with me every day of my life, here I feel them so much more intensely. Auschwitz is a place that demands from me the burden of memory."

In an interview for the documentary, Professor Wiesel says he was not cut out for the harsh conditions of the camps:

"I was a sickly child; not at all robust. I'm not sure why I survived, in truth, but I know that had a great deal to do with the presence of my father. His being with me is most likely what saved me and it's for him that I went on living."

Poignantly, following the death march to Buchenwald from Auschwitz, Elie's father was beaten by guards. He was later beaten by fellow inmates for food. Food scarcity was causing prisoners to turn on each other brutally and Elie's father was only one of many casualties. Shortly before the Allies brought

Germany to its knees, Elie Wiesel's father was sent to the gas chamber, so grievously injured, he could longer work. The war ended several weeks later.

For Professor Wiesel, returning to Auschwitz was an oddly enriching experience. In the interview he relates an enormous sense of gratitude. To be there in a place in which so many suffered so horribly, walking and remembering, was for him a means of sharing his experience for the betterment of the human condition.

During the course of Dr. Wiesel's tour of Auschwitz, the film crew came to the place where virtual mountains of human hair are displayed. With their brutal, pathological efficiency, the Nazis were experts at making the most of available resources and human hair, shorn from the heads of incoming prisoners, was no exception. This was sold to cloth manufacturers in Germany. When Auschwitz was liberated at the beginning of 1945, the Allies found fully 7 tons of hair, waiting for transport and sale. The display case in which some of this hair has been kept for public viewing is 67 feet in length. It stands as a testament to the pathology of the Nazis and their division of emotion from logic; compassion from obsessive efficiencies.

Professor Wiesel's life was changed forever by his time in the death machine of the Third Reich. But probably the most devastating impact the experience had on him was the loss of his deep faith. Where was God, he wondered? Why would God allow such evil to be unleashed on the world? We are not all like Job, able to find in the midst of suffering and evil a greater reason to believe. Most of us, completely overwhelmed spiritually, will no longer answer for a God we can no longer find a home in ourselves for. In the Third Reich's complex of mass murder, God simply ceased to be, for Elie Wiesel and for many others.

But even with his soul and faith in ruins, Wiesel did not hesitate to draw on his experience in the death camps to act as a messenger to humanity on behalf of a better, less violent, less hateful world. In transforming his pain into pedagogy, Elie Wiesel became an icon of human dignity.

His ceaseless efforts for peace and humanitarianism have made Elie Wiesel an inspiration for people around the world, and a living testament to the strength of the human spirit.

He insists people understand his mission exactly as it's intended:

"This is not about hate. This is about using my anger and humiliation as catalysts in which a better humanity is wrought. It's about memory as a means of ending the human evil of genocide by knowing what the signs are; understanding what conditions must exist to make it possible. We can work to ensure it stops happening."

Chapter 20: Michael Preisler - Survivor – Prisoner #22213

When interviewed, Michael makes it very clear that the survivors from these terrible camps are obligated to correct the misconceptions that people in the Western portion of the world have about what concentration camps really were, and what the people who were subjected to them went through.

In the United States, there is a common misconception that once the Jewish people were exterminated, the Polish population was next on the list of people to be extermination. This information was never mentioned, nor can it be known. In truth, over 3 million Polish citizens died during the extermination efforts of the Nazis, and most of them were Christians.

More than 250,000 Polish citizens were ripped from their houses and businesses and taken to Germany to participate in slave labor. Millions of these Polish citizens returned to their homes after being permanently disabled by Tuberculosis or similar illnesses. The polish were persecuted by every system imaginable. It didn't matter if they were men, women, or children; they were treated like common street trash.

Only a very small amount of inmates from concentration camps survived. Most of them died because of resistance movements that took hold in all of the concentration camps and sub-camps.

The former prisoners have an obligation to spread the truth, but only if they could be considered eyewitness to the inhumanities that occurred at the institutions stood for.

While concentration camps aren't an everyday topic, or one that people feel comfortable discussing, people need to remember that they actually existed. They need to remember that gas chambers actually existed and that people died in them. It is important that people remember that millions were unjustly murdered in brutal fashions for the ignorance of people who could not see beyond their own agenda.

Unfortunately, today, they attempt to lie about the history surrounding these topics and try to deny the truths. Michael says he is "an eyewitness to many horrifying moments that took place behind the barbed wire fence."

There were concentration camps numbering thousands spread throughout Germany and the surrounding area. Out of all of the concentration camps, the most infamous of the death camps was Auschwitz-Birkenau. This camp was created, along with others, in Polish land that was currently occupied by the Germans. To date, this camp is still considered the largest cemetery that was created because of a single group committing genocide. This group was the German military under Hitler's rule.

According to Michael, he spent almost four years there, first taken in at the age of 19 by arrest. He remembers the inscription "Through Work to Freedom" over the main gate.

Yet at the same time, the commandment of the camp stated that it was a concentration camp and that the only exit was through the chimney. Speaking of this, Michael then pointed to the chimneys of the crematorium.

He pointed out that this and other laws made it so they were no longer looked at as humans, but instead as numbers or property.

Everyone lived in blocks (barracks) and while each should have held 250-400 prisoners, they instead held anywhere from 500-1200 each, on average. Individuals only had a thin blanket, using their clothing as a pillow. People would often forget where they were lying if they got up to use the bathroom at night, due to the overcrowding. 3-tier bunks were then built after this to accommodate more people.

He felt that some could have died just from the experience of this transition.

"Beatings and kicks... gave us a forewarning of things to come later."

Prisoners, usually recruits from native Germany, who were assigned certain positions would then treat fellow prisoners no better than the SS. Many even killed other prisoners.

Insects would infest the blocks, due to dirty underwear, not enough water, and the lack of bed linen. Many prisoners were eliminated naturally, due to starvation, which also caused many illnesses and disease. This was enough to cause some prisoners mental anguish.

The Typical Day of a Prisoner

Every prisoner's day started at 4:30 in the morning, ending late in the evening. Depending on where the prisoner was working, the time they actually made it back to the blocks varied. They were alerted at the time they were to leave for their work assignment by orchestral music, which was made up of the camp's prisoners.

When the prisoners came back to the camp from work, they were typically covered in blood that could be their own, or could be from other prisoners they were carrying, who were dead, or dying. Typically, the bodies of the dead were put in an exact place so that evening formation and prisoner count could be completed. While it is not customary when someone dies, it was something that had to be done. Missing prisoners could cause the entire camp to be punished, leading to even more deaths.

The terrible, inhuman treatment of concentration camp prisoners, and the slave labor they were subjected to, caused the massive number of deaths in these camps. Women were forced to carry out actions that their bodies were not meant to do. The tools they were given were primitive in nature and they did not have the proper clothing to protect them from the elements, or the dangers of the work they were doing. Many prisoners did not have shoes, and the shoes that were provided did not provide adequate protection. They were abused, both physically and mentally. Those who could no longer carry out their duties were beaten with the butts of guns, further weakening them.

The harsh circumstances of the camp were made worse by starvation, small rations, fatigue, and constant fear of death. Because of this, prisoners had digestive disorders and diseases, bone disease, circulatory issues, respiratory issues, typhus, malaria, and more.

"The camp hospital at Auschwitz was one experimental station using human beings for various experiments."

In 1942, Michael contracted typhus fever, but was saved by a hospital medic. This was not a common practice, but since one of the other prisoners knew the medic, an exception was made.

Sleeping Quarters In the Hospital Block

Prisoners were forced to sleep five people to one bed. At least one person died each day. At times, sick prisoners were laying next to another prisoner who had recently died.

More From Michael Preisler:

Michael believes that God helped him survive through the typhus without being medicated, as his temperature returned to normal in only a few days. The recovery block he was transferred to afterward had no clothing and was terribly crowded with very few rations. Prisoners were covered with lice and ticks. He was down to 100 pounds and those described as "musulman" (mummy-like) weren't allowed in other camp areas. He made it his mission to get out of the hospital and felt others had the same feelings.

When the SS needed volunteers to work with disinfecting prisoners, Michael was called upon and given clothing. He then reported to the head of the block the next morning as a German, wearing those clothes. He stated that he'd like to be released from the hospital so that he could return to the camp. His number was then added to the list of those being released, as he had on clothing and his bones were no longer showing.

During this type of transfer, a prisoner had to stand naked front of the SS camp doctor. Then, the acceptance or refusal would occur. On the day of Michael's transfer, said doctor never showed up, so those in the transfer group were approved without an inspection, submerged in water, and received disinfected clothing. The following day, the remaining recovery block patients were taken away to be gassed, including the fit ones. In the days following, prisoners of every nationality began to be ordered to raise their pant legs to determine whether they were healthy enough to work or not and separated into groups. One group would be led to the gas chamber. Only the one German prisoner was left out of this ritual.

Gas chambers weren't the only means of killing. Some were injected with gasoline or locked in the Starvation Death Bunker. For each prisoner that fled, 10-20 more were specifically chosen by the Commander and locked in this bunker to die from famine. During one of these formations, a prisoner asked to survive because of his wife and children. A volunteer came forward and stated his reason for wanting to take this person's place instead was that he was a Catholic Priest. This man was Maximilian Kolbe, a Franciscan. He ended up surviving fifteen days deprived of food or water and then died from being injected with phenol on that 15th day.

Some prisoners were also killed by execution. Their numbers would be read out and they would then be taken by guard of the SS to block No. 11 (the death block). They would be detained for around a couple hours and then be shot in the head, with the bodies being placed on wagons with blankets over them and removed by prisoners elected as nurses. The carts were followed by a line of blood. Hangings were also done before the prisoners. This was usually done to those attempting to escape.

Amid the chaos and deplorable conditions, there was an prearranged movement to keep what was going on under wraps. In September of 1944, "Plan Molla", a plan to destroy Auschwitz and massacre all of its prisoners, was developed. This information was dispatched from camp members to the Polish anti-establishment to London, where it was then broadcast publicly. The camp then ceased "Plan Molla" and started to disband the extermination complexes.

Prisoners were evacuated by the Germans via foot columns and trains, alternating routes. Michael was evacuated from Auschwitz in January of 1945 on foot. He had on very light prison clothing, no food, and it was cold and snowing. By the time the American and British troops were able to get in to liberate the prisoners from the camps to evacuate prisoners, it was too late for entirely too many people. Even after reinforcements arrived and took the sick and wounded to hospitals and care centers, the death toll kept rising. This is because there were so many concentration camp prisoners who were in the advanced stages of malnourished and riddled with disease that many of them were care and comfort only. All the allies could do is make them comfortable and ensure that they were not alone in their final hours of life. This was especially heart breaking because many of them had already lost their families to the torment faced in the death camps and those who still had family, had no way of knowing their location. Half of the people in his column never made it to the final destination and human bodies were lying in blood amid the white snow. According to Michael, only the "strongest survived the march, but we left thousands behind us along the way."

Removing the Dead – A Convicted Guard's Duty

For the female guards who were not hanged or executed, one of their punishments were to face the indignity of their actions once again. Women were forced by the court system and the government to remove the deceased prisoners from their huts.

In total, there were 17 thousand bodies in the camp by the time the British government arrived to liberate the prisoners and set them free. Over the next several weeks, an additional 13 thousand bodies needed to be removed from their death chamber huts.

On several occasions, the female guards complained and vomited due to the smell and thought of the bodies that were so decomposed, they were barely recognizable. Because their bodies were dead weight, and they were severely decomposed due to the heat, as the nurses lifted bodies, the legs and arms would dislocate and pull from the body. They were forced to carry all of the deceased to burial pits. The female guards felt that this act was horribly traumatic. Some even developed Post Traumatic Stress Disorder because they were forced to face what they had done. Nearly 60 years later, a female officer was interviewed about the experience of removing the bodies from the huts. Her chief complaint was that the British soldiers would not allow them to wear gloves as they moved the deceased. According to the British military, if these guards were willing to stand by and watch these people suffer and starve to death, and then allow them to lay inside the huts to decompose, their punishment of removing the bodies with their bare hands was very fitting.

Nowadays, many are saying that the holocaust never happened and that there were no death camps or gas chambers. However, Michael tells another story about how Auschwitz "is a symbol of martyrdom of the Polish nation." He believes that in leaving the camp, he left behind the world's biggest cemetery that has no grave markers. According to him, the names of those who died "are only known to God." He says we should pay homage to "all innocent victims of this Holocaust tragedy... no exception as to nationality nor religion."

Pope John Paul II June 7, 1979

Comparing the nameless tombs to that of the Unknown Soldier, Pope John Paul II says: "I have come and I kneel on this Golgotha of the modern world"

He goes on to talk about kneeling before every inscription in the memory of all the victims of Auschwitz in all of their languages and calls each one out: Polish, English, Bulgarian, Romany, Czech, Danish, French, Greek, Hebrew, Yiddish, Spanish, Flemish, Servo-Croat, German, Norwegian, Russian, Romanian, Hungarian and Italian.

Pope John Paul II was speaking as a Polish Roman Catholic survivor of Auschwitz, stating he is "-an eyewitness to history... a victim in one of mankind's ugliest moments..." and wishes to speak the truth about what went on. He felt it important to say that while the topic is unpleasant, the world should be reminded that the camps did in fact exist and the "gas chambers were real, and that millions of people were murdered in a brutal way."

Chapter 21: Eugene Black – Prisoner # 55546

Eugene Black was born in 1928 to an extremely happy family. He had three sisters and one brother. His mother was born into a family of orthodox Jews, but his father was not. His father was a tailor, who lived an extremely busy life. Even though Eugene was considered Jewish, religion was really part of his upbringing.

The area where Eugene's family lived was given back to Hungary in November of 1938, but his family did not believe their lives would change very much. German forces completely took over Hungary on March 19th 1944 and his family's life took a turn for the worse. As soon as German forces took over, all members of the Jewish faith were ordered to wear a marker to signify their religion. The marker was the Star of David. Within 10 days of this order being given, everyone of Jewish faith was forced to move into the ghetto. Since Eugene already lived in the ghetto area, his family took in other Jewish families who had nowhere to go.

When Eugene was on his way home from school on May 14th, he saw a police truck sitting about 200 yards from his home. There were German military outside of his home and he noticed that the police had his two sisters and his father in the truck. He witnessed a police officer strike his mother across the face and shove her into the truck. Despite his best efforts to get into the house, the police refused to allow him in. Instead, they tossed him in the truck with the rest of his family. Once inside, he realized that the rest of the Jewish people from his ghetto were already inside.

The truck was driven to a brickyard that was nearby.

There, Eugene realized that there was a large amount of the Jewish population from where he lived being herded onto a railway train like cattle where they would later be transported to Auschwitz Birkenau. Even though he was a child, Eugene was quickly taken from his mother and his sisters, and later his father was taken too.

Once they were separated, their heads were shaved and they were showered. Eugene was given his number, 55546, and provided with the assigned striped uniform.

Eugene remembers being at Auschwitz Birkenau for approximately ten days. At this point, he was selected for slave labor. They loaded him on a train and sent him to the "Little Camp at Buchenwald." After this trip, he was moved to "Dora Mittelbau in the Harz mountains" This is the location where Nazis used slave labors to manufacture V1 and V2 rockets.

The job that Eugene was given was to load rocks into small trucks that were dug out from the tunnels. He worked 12 to 14 hour days. He was given starvation rations and was not allowed to have breaks.

After approximately five months of working at this pace, Eugene became extremely ill and was diagnosed with pneumonia. Luckily, a German doctor saved his life and he was able to recover.

In mid March of 1945, Eugene was transferred to Bergen Belsen, which he describes as "a hellhole." According to Eugene, Typhus was rampant through the camp and there were people laying everywhere. There was little to no sanitation.

April 15th liberation finally came in the form of the British Army taking over the camp. While Eugene was excited that his life had been saved, heartbreak set in when he realized that his entire family had, other than his older brother, an officer of the Czech army, was killed.

Eugene was homeless and stateless. He was only 17 years old, so he became an interpreter for the British army in Sennelager. This is where he met his wife Annie and later had four children of his own. Annie and his children gave Eugene exactly what he was looking for, a positive future.

In 1949, Eugene and his family moved to England where he began working at Marks and Spencer in their warehouse. By the time he filed for retirement, he had worked his way up to manager.

Eugene and his family now live in Leeds and he speaks openly about his experience in the camps he lives in. He makes open appearances in schools, prisons and community organizations.

Like most survivors, Eugene is still putting his family history back together. He did find out that his sisters did not die in the gas chambers, as he had believed for more than 60 years. It turns out that his sisters had been sentenced to slave labor, producing fuel for the Nazi war effort. On September 11, 1944, this factory was bombed, killing over 151 Jewish women, including his sisters. The only relief that he gets from learning the truth is that his sisters Paula and Jolan died together and are buried together. They were never alone.

Eugene has been to   to visit his sisters' graves.

Chapter 22: Trude Silman – Child Holocaust Survivor

Trude Silman was a 9 year old girl that grew up in the Czechoslovakia capital of Bratislava. She escaped to England with her cousin and aunt on a train. She grew up in and out of multiple foster homes.

Trude's real name was Gertrude Feldmann and she was born in Bratislava, right outside of the capital city. She was born the year of the Wall Street Crash and had 2 other siblings. She spent her time like any other child playing and walking through the hills. She even went tobogganing and skating during the winter months. She learned three languages at home and took ballet lessons. Her extended family such as her aunts and uncles supplied her and her family with treats and holiday festivities during the Holocaust. Trude went to a school that was dedicated to Jewish children, thanks to the laws that were instated by Hitler. Even though she does not remember experiencing any anti-Semitism as a child, it does not mean her family did not experience it at some point.

Trude only has limited memories of when Hitler rose to power, and of what Germany became. She does remember him shouting speeches over the radio. She remembers hearing her sisters and her dad being treated badly and being beaten by Nazis.

She also remembers that in 1938, everything became extremely tense around her house and when they would go grocery shopping, and after a few months, her dad made the rest of her family go to live with her grandma for safety reasons. The place they were staying was a beautiful home near the country side. Trude was able to see things she had never witnessed before since she lived in the city.

In October, the Prime Minister of Britain took a trip and visited Hitler. The reason for his visit was to stop the problems that the people of Jewish religion. Soon, Trude realized that her parents were trying to get all of her siblings and themselves out of Germany and into Czechoslovakia so they would be safe.

On December 31, 1938, Trude's sister left for her trip. She went to England to live with a family around Kew Gardens, which is close to London. The entire family traveled to visit her in May of 1939. Even though she was young, Trude realized that there was a lot of danger for her family. Her older brother found a Job in London in 1939 and she also remembers being sent home from school the same year. Looking back, the time that all of this was occurring was when Germany invaded Slovakia.

She does not have very clear memories of the trauma involved in leaving home. She does remember moving when her aunt received permission to work in England as a personal servant. She remembers clearly that her aunt took her, and her own daughter with her to England to work.

She has vague memories of them packing a taxi as tightly as possible so that they would have everything they needed. Even at the age of nine, she remembers riding in a taxi they could barely move in, as well riding on a train for at least four days. During this train ride, they were stopped countless times. Toward the end of their journey, they took a wonderful boat and had a chance to enjoy the water, after which, they road another train to Liverpool street station, where they arrived around midnight.

The first few months in England made Trude extremely homesick. The food was unfamiliar, it was cold, the houses were drafty and it was a completely different world for a child who did not speak English. To top that off, her family had just fallen completely apart through no fault of their own.
The best part of the situation was that the foster families that she lived with

showed such compassion for a child who had been through brutal hell and they did their best to help her deal with the trauma that she had dealt with at such a young age.

After a while, Trude was able to return to London and allowed to stay with her aunt and uncle while they awaited passage to America. Unfortunately, they were evacuated again to a safe place where she could stay out of the danger of the war that was breaking out all over Europe.

Luckily she was able to stay near her siblings. They were able to safely send letters to one another and their parents through the Red Cross. Sometimes the letters took 5 months to make it to their destination, but this was mostly because of safety protocols.

Over time, Trude developed a love of learning and developed a passion for science. When she was old enough, she moved to attend Leeds University and met her husband Norman there. Her brother and sister got married as well. While Trude did not give up on the search for her parents, the story does not end well.

Trude's father died in Auschwitz and 72 years later, her mother has yet to be found. She is still looking for any information about where her mother ended up. She has come to terms with the fact that her mother is deceased, but being able to visit her grave site would bring closure that she still has yet to find.

Because of her experiences and what her family went through, Trude is an extremely active member of multiple volunteer groups. She hopes to spread the word of tolerance and hope to school children so that no one ever has to face the intolerance that she did when she was a child.

Chapter 23: Random Account – Excerpts

These accounts do not contain names. Why? Because we want to make an impact by showing you what it is like to relate to other people, without their names. When people entered concentration camps, they lost their names. They were simply numbers. These numbers were tattooed onto their arms in a brutal, archaic fashion.

November 16, 1938 – Account 1

Arriving at the concentration camp, our names were called for registration purposes. We stood in line from approximately 5 in the morning until around mid-afternoon. We didn't dare move out of line. To do so would mean being kicked, punched, or hit in the head with the butt of a riffle.

We were not allowed to use the restroom and requests were met with the most horrible of verbal or physical abuse. At noon, a senior officer decided that we could be taken, as a group, to the restroom.

We were not fed until 24 hours after we had arrived. Even if it was actually horrible, the food tasted extremely good. We were starving.

At this point, our clothing was taken. We were given ragged, torn clothes that were meant for use in the concentration camp. These pieces of clothing were threadbare, old uniforms that the army had no use for any longer. It was thoroughly explained to us that were were not allowed to purchase anything from the canteen or buy a single item for ourselves. What we were given, is all we were allowed to have.

The next day, we had drill exercises. For the younger members, these exercises were easier, especially since many of us had been soldiers before our arrest. However, older men could not handle the horrible abuse. They would collapse in exhaustion. When they did, they were kicked, punched, slapped and beaten with the butts of rifles. These beatings were always accompanied by insults, vulgar language and obscene words.

There were several men who were over 70 years old. They were mistreated repeatedly during drills. When they were abused, they would fall onto their faces. At th is point, guards trampled on their backs with their hobnailed boots.

After this, roll-call was taken. During this routine, repeated insults were thrown at people without provocation. These were just the horrors of the first 48 hours in the concentration camps.

November 11, 1938 - Account 2

At 5:30 on Friday morning, I was instructed by the local police station to accompany them immediately. According to the information they provided, there was a passport inspection. Everyone was automatically paranoid about the situation, this has never happened before. We could see what was going on at the police station, I lived next door after all.

Because of the situation, I asked the police officer whether he could grab a few things from inside my house for me. He rudely refused. I called Papa immediately so that he could let Netti know what was going on. They brought me clothing as soon as they could. They also brought food. The food was taken in trucks from there, all the way to the station.

It total, there were about 2,000 people.

We left the station between 2:30 and 3:00 pm. We reached the boarder at about midnight. We were not allowed near the window of the train and we were not allowed to leave the train, even when it stopped; the doors were locked. If we were to go near the window, we were threatened with rifles, and the rifles were guaranteed to be loaded.

When we reached the boarder, officials were completely surprised. They had not been notified that the transport was happening at all. All of the German officers had disappeared (at least 200 men). They were no where to be found at all.

The entire journey, we were treated like criminals. We felt disgraced.

We waited until three in the morning. Our passports were rigorously examined and stamped. There were no arrangements for sleeping quarters or for us to eat. We had 2,000 people staying in two rooms from Friday until Monday. You could never imagine what it was like to live like this.

The atmosphere was suffocating and within those two days, four people had died. We were not allowed to have any cameras and no one was allowed to send pictures outside of our rooms.

No one was allowed to have money or food. Everyone was becoming sick from exhaustion.

Undated – Account 3

It was November 10th, around 3:30 in the morning when the telephone rang. I was warned to avoid staying in the flat because I would be arrested the second I was found. I immediately left my apartment with my son and wife. We wandered around the streets hoping not to be found.

Along the way, I ran into the banker's wife. She was wondering around the streets as well. She was dressed in the shabbiest of clothes I had ever seen her in. We also encountered a large number of Jews who were being escorted by the police and were obviously under arrest.

It was obvious that all of the windows of Jewish people were lit by lights, and police officers were standing guard outside and were armed with loaded guns. When we returned to our apartment, nothing had been stolen. However, everything had been vandalized, destroyed, slashed, ripped apart, smashed and torn apart.

We were eventually arrested at the station and we were taken to the prison gym where more than 100 other Jewish citizens were being held. At least six of these people were injured. I saw an 80 year old man with a bandaged head, since a bowl had been broken on it upon his arrest.

I also saw a rabbi who was about 60 years old. There was another man of at least 77 years old. I was released after about 10 hours, since I had a visa for the United States and I was a front line officer in the military.

November 27, 1938- Account 5

At three in the morning, the house I lived in contained a small business owned by a Jewish family. The building began to shake. The windows were shattered and the contents of the business were ruined.

Since I sleep with the windows open for ventilation, I was able to hear the ruckus from downstairs. In the building next to me, I heard a second invasion that was similar in nature.

I could see small cars pass by and two men who were wearing civilian clothing. They got out of the car and smashed the windows. Obviously, the bombardment was carefully planned. They jumped back in their car and went to the next house they planned to attack.

Around 6 AM, another convoy arrived that destroyed everything they could find. They went on a three hour destruction path. You could hear fire engines rushing up and down the streets. The smoke from fires was beginning to take over the air.

We came to learn that this action was ordered by Hitler, and was carried out by Hitler Youth who were wearing civilian clothing. The men were against what they were doing and because of this, they had been drinking until at least three in the morning to bring themselves to carry out the actions they were ordered to commit.

The next day citizens witnessed a horrible sight. The smoldering synagogues, demolished homes and blood covering the streets.

Undated- Account 6

The events in Germany, I want to express what I experienced on the nights of November 9th and 10th.

Around midnight, my phone rang. It was a man who asked me if he could stay with me. He said that something horrible had happened and that he needed somewhere to stay immediately. I of course agreed to this and he arrived disheveled, pale and shaken. He had not hat or coat, even though it was cold outside. Then, he began to tell me what had happened.

The man was in a Jewish café when a group of young men stormed the café armed with revolvers and yelling 'Revenge for Paris!' Within a fraction of a second, the youths started shooting and vandalizing the café. Luckily, the man managed to escape unharmed. I supposedly heard that the owner of the Jewish café succumbed to the injuries of the gunshot wounds inflicted on him during the shooting. The man witnessed the killing of the Jewish café owner and was terribly horrified. Luckily, the man escaped and found himself on the streets. Once in the Konigsallee which is the main street in D, the man witnessed similar vandalism acts from another group in the streets. They were vandalizing a fashion salon by smashing the windows while chanting words against the killing in Paris. 'Hang the Jews from the tree,' is what the law breakers were chanting in the streets while vandalizing properties believed to be owned by the Jewish community.

I wanted to host the man for one night but he requested me to let him go home. It was natural for me to assist the man and have him spend the night and assure him of his safety but he opted to proceed to his home. The man had just left when I had bangs and commotions from the house next door. I did not think that the attackers would resolve in taking their fight and destruction that far. I heard a crowd of rowdy youths shouting and chanting, 'Right now let's get this house and these families!' the rowdy youths intended to come and continue with their destruction in my apartment. I therefore locked the main doors and my bedroom door. I latter took my son and locked ourselves in the bathroom due to the tension and fear inflicted by the chaos and young men.

Undated –Account 7

The rowdy youths and mob of young men are everywhere. They seem happy after attaining their feat and have no regrets to the destruction caused on property and death of innocent people. There are numerous families that were robbed off properties and more than 16 people resulted in hiding and cramming in a small room for three days wishing that the skirmishes would settle down and their lives spared. The money and jewelry belonging to the Jewish community were taken away by the young men irrespective of the meaning of the valuables to the Jewish community. It was so sad that youths could tear up the earrings from children and coins from the ladies' handbags. The people that I relate with had varying explanations about the outcomes of the ordeal. They had undergone various modes of suffering in the hands of their oppressors. Although some people had taken part as soldiers in several wars, they confessed that they had never encountered such an ugly and inhumane ordeal. Below are some of the ordeals that were witnessed in the cellars that Jews were imprisoned.

50-55 year old women who were imprisoned together with men were forced to strip and dance for their fellow inmates. The scenes from the prisons clearly indicate of the levels of brutality exposed to the Jewish women and tradition. The SA had the mandate of demonstrating the dancing to the Jewish women. The sick women were never left behind in the humiliation ordeal in the prison. They were forced to answer the calls of nature in front of other inmates regardless of gender. One WC was in operation for use for approximately 200 inmates detained in a cell where they were mixed women, men and children. The children that were below 2 years were taken in prison together with their mothers and were denied food for two days. So much segregation and inhumane actions were witnessed during this period but space and time is not available to express the outcomes of the war.

December 15, 1938- Account 8

The statement is derived from the 'Children's Committee' from a 17 year old teenager from Amsterdam

I would like to portray my grievances briefly as a result of our experiences over the past few weeks. My parents, siblings and I have been in search of a sustainable way of making a living with no vain. We have been subjected to poverty due to the lack of food and modes of sustainability. We would bear our conditions due to the fact that we had promising hopes of migrating to greener and better places. We were supposed to be evicted from our current premises by the end of 31st January which was seven weeks from the current date. There were no symptoms of improvement in the near future thus we never knew what the future held for us.

Our situation turned for the worst after the detention of my father in a private and confidential place for the past five weeks. Due to the ongoing disparities between our family and success, my mother was subjected to a severe breakdown which affected our family greatly. The medication receipts and forms can be produced to ascertain on the level of sickness that my mother had been subjected to.

Can you fully understand and comprehend the reason behind our request for assistance? Do you have an idea of the impacts generated on the innocent souls of the young ones? Can you see the need to assist our family and others undergoing the same ordeal? I solemnly beseech you all in the name of my sisters and brothers and in the name of my parents to offer us your assistance and support. Kindly help!

November 10, 1938- Account 9

We discussed the happenings in Paris on 10th November evening and decided to bring home our son soonest.

Frau Adler who is my wife's sister rang us at around 2am in the morning explaining how Nazis had stormed her flat demanding to know the whereabouts of Wilhelm Adler, her father. She had apparently informed the Nazis that my step father was with us and saw it wise to warn us. Her words became evident after one hour when our door bell rang and I heard men yelling and cursing at our door step. The operation was similar to the burglaries conducted in homes by raiders. We therefore ran to the close balconies and started shouting for assistance for help. The attackers had accessed our garden and warned us to stop shouting or they would be forced to shoot.

I tried calling for help from the police but when I confirmed that the raid was being conducted in a home which was inhabited by people from the Jewish origin, the policeman said he was aware of the attack and he hang up. The criminals broke into our house and into the room that we had quietly hidden whereas my father in law jumped from the balcony into the ground floor flat. Our fate lay on the hands of the criminals.

Undated –Account 10

The destruction of religious places and objects lead me to the arrangement of the removal of the Torah scrolls and other religious related objects from the synagogue on 9th November 1938. The religious scrolls and objects were safe when the synagogue was destroyed the following day.

Pogrom night:

At around 2 am in the night of 9th and 10th November, two men broke into my apartment and threatened Christians with guns. Similarly, I was protected by two men with guns and after more than 11 men stole and destroyed everything, they left assuring me that they had been mandated to protect and defend me from any kind of oppression.

The theft was carefully crafted since jewelry, camera, typewriter, cash, artworks, household silver and my briefcases were all gone. Nothing fragile was left intact including pictures and drawings. After the departure of the thieves, my cousin came to collect me and take me home but we learnt on the plans of arresting Jewish men. My cousin therefore ran away to Holland and later relocated to USA.

Chapter 24: People From Both Sides Recount Their Holocaust – Short Stories

Melita Maschmann

Bund Deutscher Madel Member

I did not see anything occurring during the riots of Crystal Night on November 9, 1938. When I woke up the following morning I laid my eyes upon the wreckage in Alexanderplatz. These wrecked restaurants and shops were where the Jews inhabited.

We always heard that international jury was always trying to stir the world up against Germany. Now a petrifying warning was given to the Jews. This warning horrified me seeing the violence all over the streets.

I wondered what the people that owned these small shops had done to affect the international Jewish capitalist that ended in their shops being destroyed. Because of the sorrow that was caused to these innocent people I tried to block out these times as fast as possible.

It was easier to jump back into work than to keep thinking about these things.

Emmy Bonhoeffer

Sister-in-law of German Resistance Martyr Pastor Dietrich Bonhoeffer

When I was out and about one day I talked to a neighbor of mine telling him that they were killing Jews that were locked in outdoor concentration camps and were making soap out of them.

My neighbor told me back that I would end up in one of those camps for telling horror stories that are so awful and if they take me they would not be able to help me. What you are telling people is not true and you should not believe everything you hear. The international radio broadcasts are trying just making more enemies for our country to deal with by telling us such stories.

On the way home, I turned I looked at my husband. He was not amused at all about what I had said. He looked at me and told me, "My dear, sorry to say but you are absolutely idiotic what you are doing. Please understand the dictatorship is like a snake."

"If you put a foot on its tail, as you do, it will bite you. You have to strike the head and you can't do that, neither you or I can do that. The only single way is to convince the military who have the arms to do it, to convince them that they have to act, that they have to make a coup d'etat."

Hertha Beese

Berlin Housewife and Social Democrat

There was very religious family of Jewish faith that lived in an apartment under us. They were safe from being taken and persecuted because the dad was of Italian descent and was in the Mussolini group.

Even with the father having his Italian connection the wife still thought they would come and take her, never to be seen again. Because of this she became scared and insecure and she left.

Soon the flat under us was barren. I begged the landlord to not fill it again. I wanted it to stay empty in the chance that there was a full collapse and our difficulties would be gone.

I would look after the flat while it was empty. One night there was a doorbell that went off at about midnight. When I opened the door there stood a couple, who just happened to be of Jewish faith. At this moment, I started helping the persecuted Jews. I was now part of the circle of invisible people who would hide and smuggle Jews.

I passed them around if there was a hiding place that had been found. They only traveled at night where it was much harder to see them. I never did find out how or who told them how to find me

Problems started to occur when feeding the Jewish started to become difficult. They mostly did not feed the people of Jewish faith because they did not have their rationing cards or money. Because of this, many were forced to trade potatoes and bread for smoking cards, or ask a friend to give them small amounts of the meager rations they did get. Since this was illegal, those who did this had to keep their sources and the names of those helping them secret at all costs.

Rita Boas- Koupmann

Dutch –Jewish Teenager survivor of Auschwitz – Birkenau

"I think the alarm started when Jewish people had their card with a "J" on it."

Conclusion

On January 27th, 1945, the Soviet Red Army liberated Auschwitz. The Soviets had discovered other camps, but nothing prepared them for Auschwitz, and nothing prepared the world for it.

When the camp was liberated, there were an estimated 7,000 people left alive. Many of these would die in the coming days, from starvation, exposure, weakness, and disease. Many were children who had arrived on the last transports to the camp. Most of them had escaped the last murderous orgy of the SS before the Nazis had fled the camp – probably only the Soviets' advance, much more rapid than previously believed, saved them.

Over the last few weeks, the gassing process had almost ceased at Auschwitz, and the remaining crematoria had been blown up. Two had been destroyed or damaged in a prisoner revolt in October 1944, in which three SS guards were killed and over 200 prisoners lost their lives. Thousands of inmates were forcibly marched deeper behind German lines to other camps. Those who could not keep up were shot along the roadside. These "death marches," which came not only from Auschwitz, but from other camps in the east, resulted in tens of thousands of deaths.

When the Soviets entered the camp, they found evidence of the mass slaughter that the Nazis had not managed to destroy and they found the children. The children liberated from Auschwitz and other camps are very old now, and there are few survivors left. There are numerous organizations throughout the United States and Europe that can put you in touch with survivors that are all too willing to tell their stories to you so that you will be one of the people who can give testimony after they are gone.

January 1945.

Finally, we would like to ask you to give a short, honest, and unbiased review of this book.

Click HERE to leave a Review.

Please & Thank you!

Check Out My Other Books

Below you'll find some of my other popular books that are listed on Amazon and Kindle as well. Simply click on the links below to check them out. Alternatively, you can click on my author name here ->"Ryan Jenkins" on Amazon to see other work done by me.

- Irma Grese & Other Infamous SS Female Guards
- World War 2: A Brief History of the European Theatre
- World War 2 Pacific Theatre: A Brief History of the Pacific Theatre
- World War 2 Nazi Germany: The Secrets of Nazi Germany in World War II
- The Third Reich: The Rise & Fall of Hitler's Germany in World War 2
- World War 2 Soldier Stories: The Untold Stories of the Soldiers on the Battlefields of WWII
- World War 2 Soldier Stories Part II: More Untold Tales of the Soldiers on the Battlefields of WWII
- Surviving the Holocaust: The Tales of Survivors and Victims
- World War 2 Heroes: Medal of Honor Recipients in WWII & Their Heroic Stories of Bravery
- World War 2 Heroes: WWII UK's SAS hero Robert Blair "Paddy" Mayne
- World War 2 Heroes: Jean Moulin & the French Resistance Forces
- World War 2 Snipers: WWII Famous Snipers & Sniper Battles Revealed
- World War 2 Spies & Espionage: The Secret Missions of Spies & Espionage in WWII

- World War 2 Air Battles: The Famous Air Combat that Defined WWII
- World War 2 Tank Battles: The Famous Tank Battles that Defined WWII
- World War 2 Famous Battles: D-Day and the Invasion of Normandy
- World War 2 Submarine Stores: True Stories from the Underwater Battlegrounds
- The Holocaust Saviors: True Stories of Rescuers who risked all to Save Holocaust Refugees
- Irma Grese & The Holocaust: The Secrets of the Blonde Beast of Auschwitz Exposed
- Auschwitz & the Holocaust: Eyewitness Accounts from Auschwitz Prisoners & Survivors

- World War 2 Sailor Stories: Tales from Our Warriors at Sea
- World War 2 Soldier Stories Part III: The Untold Stories of German Soldiers
- World War 2 Navy SEALs: True Stories from the First Navy SEALs: The Amphibious Scout & Raiders

If these links do not work for whatever reason, you can simply search for these titles on the Amazon website to find them.

Instant Access to Free Book Package!

As a thank you for the purchase of this book, I want to offer you some more material. We collaborate with multiple other authors specializing in various fields. We have best-selling, master writers in history, biographies, DIY projects, home improvement, arts & crafts and much more! **We make a promise to you to deliver at least 4 books a week in different genres, a value of $20-30, for FREE!**

All you need to do is sign up your email here at http://nextstopsuccess.net/freebooks/ to join our Book Club. You will get weekly notification for more free books, courtesy of the First Class Book Club.

As a special thank you, we don't want you to wait until next week for these 4 free books. We want to give you 4 **RIGHT NOW**.

Here's what you will be getting:

1. A fitness book called "BOSU Workout Routine Made Easy!"
2. A book on Jim Rohn, a master life coach: "The Best of Jim Rohn: Lessons for Life Changing Success"
3. A detailed biography on Conan O'Brien, a favorite late night TV show host.
4. A World War 2 Best Selling box set (2 books in 1!): "The Third Reich: Nazi Rise & Fall + World War 2: The Untold Secrets of Nazi Germany".

To get instant access to this free ebook package (a value of $25), and weekly free material, all you need to do is click the link below:

http://nextstopsuccess.net/freebooks/

Add us on Facebook: First Class Book Club

Printed in Poland
by Amazon Fulfillment
Poland Sp. z o.o., Wrocław